The Couple's Adventure

OVER 200 IDEAS TO SEE, HEAR, TASTE, AND TRY IN CENTRAL FLORIDA

K V A A L A™

"

Create moments and memories with your loved one. Coming out of your comfort zone and experiencing new things will be more rewarding and life-changing than just owning new things.

Table of Contents

INTRODUCTION   01

CHAPTER ONE – 50 IDEAS TO SEE IN CENTRAL FLORIDA   03

From lush natural parks teeming with the flora and fauna that Florida's famous for to the Orlando space center, Central Florida has plenty of amazing things to marvel at. Come see our picks for things that you and your significant other can see in the central part of the state.

CHAPTER TWO – 11 IDEAS TO HEAR IN CENTRAL FLORIDA   55

Whether it's a night of smooth jazz or a head-banging concert in one of Central Florida's innumerable venues, there's plenty for a couple to go hear in this region of the state. Check out our listings for the best things for a couple to hear, and go share a memorable experience with your loved one!

CHAPTER THREE – 69 IDEAS TO TASTE IN CENTRAL FLORIDA   67

There's no shortage of marvelous restaurants in this vacation state, where the best culinary traditions from the Caribbean and beyond blend with American ingenuity and passion to create memorable dining experiences. Whether you and your date are looking for a fancy night on the town, or just a bite on the road in Central Florida, we've got you covered!

CHAPTER FOUR – 81 IDEAS TO TRY IN CENTRAL FLORIDA   137

Looking for something more adventurous? We've found dozens of great activities for you to try in the heart of the Everglade State. From thrilling physical activities that will get your pulse racing to quieter things you and your partner can do together; we've got things for you to try in Central Florida that will make your vacation a special one.

CONCLUSION   219

INTRODUCTION

F lorida - The Everglade State – has long been one of America's top vacation destinations. Its miles of sunny coastline, beautiful natural areas, and booming metropolises mean that it's got pretty much any type of attraction, natural or manmade, that you can think of. That's why we put together this e-book guide for you and your loved one. While COVID-19 has made it difficult for many Americans to travel outside of their home state today, there are plenty of gems that abound right in your own state. If that home state happens to be Florida, or if you're able to travel there, then we're about to provide you with more than 200 incredible things you can see, hear, taste, and try in the central part of this magnificent state.

As you know, some of the best-hidden spots in any given area aren't easily found online. You won't always find them on Instagram; even locals might not even know about them. You need an intimate, tell-all guide that's going to not only guide you to fun and exciting adventures, but also an experience that's perfect for couples seeking a romantic getaway. Nothing is more bonding then going on a trip with the person who means the most to you. The experiences you'll share, seeing new lands and sights together, will be memories that'll last a lifetime.

We've organized these attractions by category. First, we'll share things you can see, followed by things you can hear, things to taste, and finally experiences to try. We've broken down the listings by sense so you can easily flip to the kind of activity you and your significant other want to do that day. We've spent careful time researching these ideas so that you can enjoy whatever trip, adventure, or exploration is just right for you and your partner.

We have, to the best of our ability, provided you with all the details you need to know regarding our listings. Of course, if you ever have any questions or need any clarification, please do not hesitate to reach out to our team.

If you enjoy our suggestions, we'd love it if you took the time to leave us a review on Amazon!

COVID-19 DISCLAIMER

Due to the COVID-19 social distancing mandates, some of the following suggestions may be temporarily closed for access or viewing. We recommend that you visit their websites and social media accounts to check on the status of reopening. Some sites may have adjusted hours as well. Please review before visiting the location. Thank you!

NEW RELEASES

Make sure you subscribe on www.eepurl.com/hcUWDb to be notified when we publish a new book with more things to see, hear, taste or try.

So, without further ado, let's dive into: *The Couple's Adventure – Over 200 Ideas to See, Hear, Taste, and Try in Central Florida.*

CHAPTER ONE
50 Ideas to See in Central Florida

From lush natural parks teeming with the flora and fauna that Florida's famous for to the Orlando space center, Central Florida has plenty of amazing things to marvel at. Come see our picks for things that you and your significant other can see in the central part of the state.

01

Imagine yourselves in a world of Glass Art

Glass art is, perhaps, one of the most underappreciated forms of expression we have. Its vibrance and diversity are too often overlooked, and those who do take the time to truly appreciate it are almost always uniquely satisfied. Don't make the mistake of overlooking this incredible artform! The Imagine Museum offers stunning artistic takes manifested as gorgeous glass-blown masterpieces. Shapes come to life, color and light playfully dance with one another, and the entire experience will feel like a magical journey. At the Imagine Museum, you will find both international and American masterpieces created by some of the world's best glass artists. This is the perfect complement to any date-night plans.

🌐 www.imaginemuseum.com

f www.facebook.com/imaginemuseumflorida

📍 1901 Central Ave., St. Petersburg, FL 33713

Go tropical at the Gizella Kopsick Palm Arboretum

The trees here are simply stunning, with more than 500 cycads and palms including nearly 150 species from every corner of the globe. This constantly growing arboretum is a continuous work in progress as the organizers call it a "never-ending project." As new types of trees become available, they will continue to be added to the display; this means that each time you revisit the arboretum you are likely to be treated to something new! There really is no better place to walk hand-in-hand with your best guy or gal than in the beauty and serenity of nature. The Gizella Kopsick Palm Arboretum is the perfect place to do so while taking in St. Petersburg.

www.stpeteparksrec.org/gizellakopsick

www.facebook.com/stpeteparksrec

North Shore Dr. & 11th Ave. NE. St. Petersburg, FL 33701

See feats of bareback derring-do at the Mosaic Rodeo Arena

Bareback riding, barrel racing, team roping, and much more are among some of the great things you will find at the Mosaic Rodeo Arena. Oh, and of course, the bull riding is nothing to scoff at, either! The arena itself is spectacular, and the Arcadia All-Florida Championship Rodeo hosted there brings some of the best talent in the business to the region. This is a unique way to enjoy the state's robust sports scene, and you may find yourself itching to hop on one of these magnificent beasts yourself! Add Mosaic in if you are a sports fan of any kind; you will not be sorry!

🌐 arcadiarodeo.com/mosaic-arena

ⓕ www.facebook.com/arcadiaallflorida.championshiprodeo

📍 2450 NE Roan St., Arcadia, FL 34266

Kiss your partner at Lake Kissimmee

You will find wildlife galore at the Lake Kissimmee State Park as it is flush with everything from bald eagles to white-tailed deer, cranes, turkeys, bobcats and more. This local gem is a prime spot for animal lovers to find some of their favorite creatures frolicking in the wild. Nestled neatly between lakes Kissimmee, Rosalie and Tiger, this is a great place for some fishing, canoeing or to simply take in some beautiful scenery. The park features six miles of equestrian trails and 13 miles of hiking paths. Of course, there are also tons of campsites open as well should you and your travel partner want to snuggle up under the stars for a romantic night under the stunning central Florida sky. And of course, with a name like Kissimmee, you're going to have to sneak in a few kisses with your sweetheart.

---

www.floridastateparks.org/parks-and-trails/lake-kissimmee-state-park

www.facebook.com/FLStateParks

14248 Camp Mack Rd., Lake Wales FL 33898

05

Aim high at the Kennedy Space Center LC-39 Observation Gantry

If you ever wanted to see "skyrockets in flight," the Kennedy Space Center LC-39 Observation Gantry is the place to do it; it is mere miles from the famed Cape Canaveral Air Force Station rocket launch pads. Watch one of modern science's most amazing feats from the shaded gantry or outdoor seating area and cozy up as the Atlas, Falcon and Delta rockets lift off nearby. You will also get to take home a souvenir and enjoy some light refreshments while you watch the magic happen. This is a one-of-kind experience that you can't get just anywhere, so if you get a chance to see a rocket launch, take it; you'll be telling your grandkids about this one for decades to come!

🌐 www.kennedyspacecenter.com/launches-and-events

f www.facebook.com/KennedySpaceCenterVisitorComplex

📍 100 Saturn Causeway, Space Center, FL 33755

Meet real live mermaids at Weeki Wachee

This state park is known for more than its nice water and hiking trails – it's a water park where you can catch real live Mermaid Shows. In an aquarium-like setting, you can watch performers wearing dazzling fish tails and other exotic costumes swim, dance, and generally enchant in an underwater theater. At 20-feet below the spring's surface, the young women are trained in the art of holding their breath for minutes at a time, to provide a spectacular show that will be thrilling and also romantic for you and your partner. The sight of beautiful mermaids swimming gracefully in the clear blue water is something you won't forget. Consider this as a whimsical, off-the-beaten-path kind of activity to add to your upcoming calendar.

www.weekiwachee.com

www.facebook.com/WeekiWacheeSprings

FL 34606

07

Take in the culture at the Dr. Phillips Center

The Dr. Phillips Center for the Performing Arts is a sprawling, magnificent complex full of beauty and wonder. Some of the most creative people in the world perform there, and it will prove to be both an enjoyable and educational experience for any visitor. The self-described "hub" of local, national and international artistry has something for visitors from every walk of life. Its two blocks of attractions include the Walt Disney Theater, the DeVos Family Room, the Dr. Phillips Center AdventHealth School of the Arts and Steinmetz Hall, and more. The center has been recognized as one of the top places to add to your "bucket list" by Travel and Leisure magazine; we are not going to argue with them. This is a great spot.

🌐 www.drphillipscenter.org/explore/about

f www.facebook.com/DrPhillipsCenter

📍 445 S. Magnolia Ave., Orlando, FL 32801

Get mesmerized at Bellydance By Jennifer Inc.

Jennifer is a pro's pro, and a multi-award-winning belly dancer that has captivated the world since she burst on the scene in 2007. Her internationally recognized dancing has garnered first place in a number of competitions worldwide and she always brings her "A" game to any wedding, birthday party or corporate gathering. Known for her charisma, creativity and "abdominal feats," she is truly a cut above the competition. With expertise in dance, event management and culture, Jennifer is a great choice for any occasion. Also, should you be interested in learning the art of belly dancing, Jennifer offers an online studio for budding dancers.

🌐 bellydancebyjennifer.com

📘 www.facebook.com/Bellydancebyjenniferinc

📍 Orlando, FL

Take in a game at Amway Center

Home to the National Basketball Association's Orlando Magic as well as the Orlando Solar Bears hockey team, the Amway Center is another big part of central Florida's massive sports market. This is a great bucket-list destination for any sports fan, and the arena itself is modern, sleek and comfortable no matter who you are rooting for. And you never know – you and your beau may even find yourselves up on the "kiss-cam" should you make it out to one of the venue's sporting events! Mix in some hoops between the gardens, museums, roller coasters and parks Orlando is known for; you may just find a little "Magic" while you are attending!

🌐 www.amwaycenter.com

f www.facebook.com/amwaycenter

📍 400 West Church St., Orlando, FL 32801

10

Go deep in The Bunker

This museum is the perfect homage to United States military members who served their nation bravely over the course of its storied history. The museum, specifically, aims at awareness, education, and the sharing of vital information about the critical role the military plays, as well as the impact war has on those who fight them. There are tons of information and displays dealing with the Vietnam War, and this is a tremendous location for military enthusiasts, history buffs and veterans to visit while in Orlando. The museum also works hard to provide assistance and support to veterans readjusting to civilian life. Stop in to honor the men and women who served America at this military history staple.

originalbunker.org

www.facebook.com/thebunkerridersorlando

3400 N Tanner Rd., Orlando, FL 32826

11

See the great Florida outdoors at Kelly Park

Just north of Orlando, Apopka's Kelly Park has all the outdoor delights you could possibly ask for in your visit to the Sunshine State. They have everything from swimming to pavilions and hiking trails galore to explore. Kelly Park is a great place to set down a cozy blanket, pour out something to drink, and dive into a picnic basket alongside your best beau. Once you are all finished, take a nice dip in the Rock Springs and cool off from a hot Florida day. Should you want to extend your stay there, they also offer tons of camp sites to throw down a sleeping bag and rough it a bit. You will not be disappointed with a romantic night under the stars at this fantastic Orange County destination!

www.ocfl.net/cultureparks/parks.aspx

400 E Kelly Park Rd, Apopka, FL 32712

12

Experience the excitement at Daytona International Speedway

Regardless of your affinity for NASCAR or not, it's a right of passage to see a NASCAR race at some point in Florida. The sight of brightly colored racecars speeding endlessly around the track is a uniquely American pastime. In particular, you must visit the Daytona International Speedway, home to the famous Daytona 500 race. What most people don't know is that the track is home to many other races throughout the year, where you can purchase tickets and tours. Take your seat in the stands at watch as NASCAR drivers rev up to 160mph, sending their vehicles hurtling around the curves at seemingly impossible speeds on a three-lap thrill ride.

🌐 www.daytonainternationalspeedway.com

f www.facebook.com/DaytonaInternationalSpeedway

📍 1801 W International Speedway Blvd, Daytona Beach, FL 32114

13

Marvel at an art deco masterwork at Bok Tower Gardens

Located in Lake Wales, Florida, the Bok Tower Gardens are regarded as one of the most beautiful carillons in the world, nestled into the top of Iron Mountain. The centerpiece amidst the lush gardens is an astonishing 205-foot neo-Gothic and Art Deco tower that was created by Milton B. Medary with the help of stone sculptor Lee Lawrie. Built with soaring graceful lines and windows with beautiful colors artfully shaped into bold geometric designs, the tower's door depicts the Book of Genesis with intricate carved details that are otherworldly. It's a uniquely American construct, echoing the historical glamor of old Europe rebuilt with a 20th century sensibility. If possible, go between 1PM and 3PM to catch the Bok gardens 60-bell carillon, which plays every day.

www.boktowergardens.org

www.facebook.com/boktowergardens

1151 Tower Blvd, Lake Wales, FL 33853

14

Witness history at the Bay Area Renaissance Festival

The Bay Area Renaissance Festival has everything you might expect from a 16th Century village including wenches, wise guys, nobility, and of course, knights in shining armor. There is music, there is dancing, and there is food fit for royalty at this fully immersive festival of yore. More than 80 artisans take part in the fair, so there will be plenty of chances to do some renaissance shopping for your significant other. You will be delighted by the many memorable characters inhabiting this European-themed town, and if you are lucky, you may even get a chance to see the regal Queen Katherine Parr with her royal court! Lords and Ladies staying in Tampa should make this a priority destination during their Florida excursions.

———————————

🌐 www.bayarearenfest.com

f www.facebook.com/bayarearenaissance

📍 11315 N. 46th St., Tampa, FL 33617

15

Come see the 'Big Top' of the Art World

The John and Mable Ringling Museum of Art is more than just a collection of artwork, although the collection is quite magnificent. They also have a circus, a theatre, a stunning garden, and so much more. There, you can explore the works of Frans Hals, Sam Gilliam, Saitō Kiyoshi and tons of other amazing and talented creators. The Ringling is a fantastic way to inject a broad range of culture into your Florida vacation as this Sarasota destination boasts one of the most impressive collections in the area. Be ready for a truly top-tier clinic in art history should you be able to make it to the John and Mable Ringling Museum of Art.

🌐 www.ringling.org

ⓕ www.facebook.com/TheRingling

📍 5401 Bay Shore Rd., Sarasota, FL 34243

Enjoy the wonders of SeaWorld Orlando

Does SeaWorld Orlando need any explaining? As one of the most impressive aquatic animal performances, zoos, and rehabilitation facilities in the world, SeaWorld is one of the best places to see everything from penguins and whales, to seals and dolphins. Admire ocean life from the comfort of an aquarium, including some whose natural environment is far from Florida. More than just a spectacle, the park is also home to rides and attractions, an aquatic waterpark, shows and presentations, and personal animal experiences. You can book a slot ahead of time to get up close and personal with your favorite animal!

🌐 www.seaworld.com/orlando

f www.facebook.com/seaworldorlando

📍 7007 SeaWorld Drive Orlando, FL 32821

17

Visit the actual Space Shuttle Atlantis

The famed shuttle is a spectacular exhibit at the Kennedy Space Center, with its signature rocket boosters and external orange tank welcoming visitors from all around the world. The shuttle is displayed exactly as it would have been in space: rotated precisely 43.21 degrees and with its payload doors wide open. This is a piece of American history that truly encapsulates the nation's space program and exploration efforts. Be sure to soak in every second of the spacecraft, which has orbited the planet more than 4,800 times during its distinguished career. There are simply not a lot of other pieces of Americana that carry the gravity of the Space Shuttle Atlantis.

🌐 www.kennedyspacecenter.com

f www.facebook.com/KennedySpaceCenterVisitorComplex

📍 Space Commerce Way, Merritt Island, FL 32953

18

Go wild at the Serengeti Safari

This magnificent 65-acre open-air tour offers adventure and excitement. You will get a close-up look at some of the most stunning African wildlife on the continent. You will also get the benefit of expert guidance during a half-hour long off-road excursion where you will have the chance to peep at ostriches, zebras, giraffes, antelope, rhinoceros and more. So, snuggle up close with your special someone and see how many of these amazing creatures you will be able to find in the Serengeti. And, of course, don't forget to bring a camera with your best zoom lens; you are going to need it at this award-winning Busch Gardens Tampa Bay attraction.

🌐 buschgardens.com/tampa/tours/serengeti-safari

ⓕ www.facebook.com/BuschGardensTampaBay

📍 10165 N McKinley Drive, Tampa, FL 33612

19

Stop and smell the roses at the Marie Selby Botanical Gardens

This is an enormous display of botanical excellence, with 15 acres of downtown space dedicated to a world-class collection of plant life. The Downtown Campus on Sarasota Bay boasts a one-of-a-kind collection of orchids, ferns and gesneriads (like the African Violet); in fact, it is the only botanical garden on the planet dedicated to the study and display of epiphytic orchids, bromeliads and other tropical plants. In other words, you'll see flowers here you won't find anywhere else. The Marie Selby Botanical Gardens Downtown Sarasota Campus also boasts a significant emphasis on botany and horticulture, and you will, without a doubt, learn something new about these incredible plants should you find yourself there. Come for the flowers, stay for the culture and history!

🌐 selby.org

f www.facebook.com/selbygardens

📍 1534 Mound St., Sarasota, FL 34236

Experience nature at
Lowry Park Zoo

Who doesn't want to pet some animals and watch them in their natural habitats on a date? The majesty of these beasts can only be appreciated in person and up close. The Lowry Park Zoo in Tampa Bay is home to more than 1,700 different animals, which makes it a full-day activity for you and your significant other to enjoy. The zoo gives you the option to interact with the animals one on one, which is not something you can count on at every zoo. Feed a towering giraffe (from a suitably high balcony, of course), pet the enormous pebbled shell of a giant tortoise, or take a picture with one of the many furry critters that's waiting to greet you.

🌐 zootampa.org

f www.facebook.com/ZooTampa

📍 1101 W Sligh Ave, Tampa, FL 33604

21

Sail across the swamp with Wild Florida Airboats

The swamps of the Everglades are a unique ecosystem, but their nature makes it hard to get around unless you have the right kind of transportation. It's time to plunge headfirst into the Headwaters of the Florida Everglades, on a wild adventure you are never going to forget. Mainly known for their airboat tours, Wild Florida offers more than just that – you can visit more than 200 native and exotic animals inside the Alligator Park, as well as enjoy a nice lunch based on swamp delicacies served at the Chomp House Grill. Glide across the plant-filled swamps on an airboat, which uses enormous fans to drive it through waters that would tangle any conventional propeller. After that, get up close and personal with the animals during one of the interactive animal encounters at the drive-thru Safari Park. You can spend the entire day at this facility.

🌐 www.wildfloridairboats.com

f www.facebook.com/Wildfloridairboats

📍 3301 Lake Cypress Rd, Kenansville, FL 34739

22

Hunt shells at Egmont Key State Park

Pristine beaches and an historical lighthouse are just some of the special features of this spectacular wildlife refuge. The white sandy shores are a great place to relax, collect gleaming colorful shells along secluded beaches, and explore all that Mother Nature has to offer you. Accessible only by private boat, the Egmont Key is a natural location with cultural history, as well as a lighthouse built almost 150 years ago. Take your time touring the historic sites and trails, while you swim in the clear blue waters, fish, and gaze at the wildlife from the marked trails. Located at the mouth of Tampa Bay, southwest of Fort DeSoto Beach, be sure to bring your camera.

🌐 www.floridastateparks.org/parks-and-trails/egmont-key-state-park

f www.facebook.com/pages/Egmont-Key-State-Park/104063009630702

📍 St. Petersburg, FL 33715

—————— **23** ——————

Let your imagination soar at the Warbird Museum

The Valiant Air Command, Inc. boasts an expansive collection of more than 50 historic warbirds collected over the 43-year history of the museum. Just a stone's throw from the Kennedy Space Center, this is a great complement for visitors looking to the skies for something amazing along Florida's east coast. Check out these amazing, restored aircraft, and even take a look at the process of how they are spruced up for display. Give the Warbird Museum a visit if you and your significant other want to see some of the most incredible ways we have learned to fly high!

——————————

🌐 www.valiantaircommand.com

f www.facebook.com/VACwarbirdairshow

📍 6600 Tico Road, Titusville, FL 32780

Dazzle yourselves at the Chihuly Collection

There is something inherently romantic about artwork—perhaps it is the relentless pursuit of beauty driving it that gives it that appeal, or maybe it is the romance of never really knowing what one means when they create something. Whatever the case, though, you will feel all of it at the Morean Arts Center, one of the state's top art destinations. Another wonderful St. Petersburg attraction, the Chihuly Collection at the Morean Arts Center is a magnificent locale for a romantic date night. Get lost in the exotic abstract glasswork of the brilliant Dale Chihuly at this can't-miss art attraction, and be sure to soak in every ounce of what he has to offer.

———————————

🌐 www.moreanartscenter.org/chihuly

f www.facebook.com/MoreanArtsCenter

📍 720 Central Avenue, St. Petersburg, FL, 33701

25

Get romantic at the Kraft Azalea Garden

Elegant is really the only way to describe the beauty of central Florida's Kraft Azalea Garden. This public garden space is more than 5 acres of pure bliss located just of off Lake Maitland's shore. It is quiet, isolated and stunning. You are definitely going to want to take a good, long hand-in-hand stroll with your best guy or gal as you meander the gardens and enjoy the shade from the garden's composing Cyprus trees. This is an especially great place to watch the sun set over Florida's gorgeous lake lands, and it also makes a pretty amazing wedding venue, too! (Wink, wink.) Take a break from the hustle and bustle of Orlando and give the Kraft Azalea Garden a visit.

cityofwinterpark.org/departments/parks-recreation

www.facebook.com/WinterParkFla

401 South Park Ave, Winter Park, FL 32789

Go wild with Amazing Animals Inc

Want to spend a day admiring the long, silky hair of a sloth suspended from a branch, marveling at the gleaming natural mosaic of a turtle shell, or staring into the wide eyes of a lemur? Amazing Animals Inc. is the place to go for a day of amazing animal sights! Established in 2009 as a federally licensed nonprofit to raise funds for offsetting the cost of reptile rehabilitation, Amazing Animals Inc. today shares their passion and love for the animals they cherish so dearly. Starting with just 30 reptiles in central Florida, over the past decade the nonprofit has grown into an educational center that travels to schools, nursing homes, and more to raise money for reptile care and protection. If you want to spend an afternoon with some of Mother Nature's most impressive creations, check out Amazing Animals Inc. today.

🌐 www.amazinganimalsinc.org

f www.facebook.com/amazinganimalsinc

📍 4235 Rambler Ave, St Cloud, FL 34772

27

Drive through the wilds at Lake Apopka

The lands surrounding Lake Apopka are an awesome place to stretch your legs and get some fresh air as the Lake Apopka Loop Trail and blazed hiking trails service bikers, walkers and even horseback riders. However, a notable highlight of the area is the 11-mile-long Wildlife Drive that really is a something to behold. The Lake Apopka Wildlife Drive runs along the easter section of the lake's adjacent lands starting at Lust Road and ending at Jones Avenue in Orange County. Plan to spend as many as three hours depending on how many stops you and your peeping companion want to make. Remember, too, motor vehicles only have access to the Wildlife Drive on Fridays through Sunday and on federal holidays. Take a half-day to see all that this incredibly diverse region has to offer.

🌐 www.sjrwmd.com/lands/recreation/lake-apopka

f www.facebook.com/sjrwmd

📍 Lake Apopka Loop Trail, Apopka, FL 32703

28

Get a unique view from the Orlando Eye

Talk about a sight you will never forget, the Orlando Eye is an air conditioned observation deck that provides you with a 360-degree of Orland and beyond. This enormous structure defies belief, a towering Ferris type wheel of gleaming white metal during the day, and a rainbow of iridescent colors at night. Experience the incomparable beauty of Orlando from 400 feet in the air as you travel around the entire circular Orlando Eye shape. There are few other ways to get such a remarkable view of the area. Reserve one of the pods for you and your significant other while you sit back, cuddle, and take in the sights around you. Be sure to bring a phone for video and a camera for pictures!

🌐 www.iconparkorlando.com

f www.facebook.com/pages/The-Orlando-Eye-Ferris-Wheel/721133957971141

📍 8375 International Dr, Orlando, FL 32819

29

Get surreal at the Dali Museum

Museums may not sound like fun to everyone, but when it comes to the Dali Museum in Saint Petersburg, Florida, you may want to think again. The famed Spanish artist Salvador Dali was cherished for his unique and unusual public persona as well as his distorted works of art. His bizarre stunts, such as walking an anteater on a leash through Paris, are just as famous as his twisted and surreal paintings, portraying disturbingly realistic hallucinogenic scenes with an astonishing degree of artistic skill and talent. The museum made in his honor allows you to explore his work further and learn about the man behind the madness. It's a great afternoon activity for you and a significant other to check out, and definitely something different from other run of the mill Florida attractions.

🌐 www.thedali.org

f www.facebook.com/thedalimuseum

📍 1 Dali Blvd, St. Petersburg, FL 33701

Take aim with the Florida Frontiersmen

For an explosive good time, visit the Florida Frontiersmen and jump back in time to an era of smithing, basketmaking, archery, and, of course, muzzle-loaded long rifles! There, you will learn all about the creativity and ingenuity of the area's first pioneers and settlers. This is a great destination in the heart of the Sunshine State, just east of Tampa in beautiful Homeland, Florida. There is a ton to see and do there. If you're historically inclined, this is a perfect off-beat date spot that's a great change of pace from the theme parks and beaches scattered throughout Florida. Come prepared for some real-deal adventure should you find yourself visiting the Florida Frontiersmen during your travels; they have a boatload of it to spare!

🌐 www.floridafrontiersmen.org

f www.facebook.com/Florida-Frontiersmen-Inc-101982821722973

📍 1000 Old Fort Meade Rd, Homeland, FL 33847

31

When the going gets tough, the tough go to the SEAL Museum

The National Navy SEAL Museum offers an up-close and personal look at one of the most fearsome fighting forces on the planet, one of the key parts of the United States Special Forces. The expansive facility honors soldiers past and present, and it works to illustrate the rich history of the SEALs with interactive exhibits, memorials, and more. The weaponry on display is impressive, the merchandise is cool, and the experience will be memorable for both military history enthusiasts and casual onlookers alike. Pay this place a visit for a one-of-a-kind look at the "quiet professionals" who have played an incredible role in the nation's history.

🌐 www.navysealmuseum.org

f www.facebook.com/NavySEALMuseum

📍 3300 N. Hwy. A1A, North Hutchinson Island, Fort Pierce, FL 34949

Soak in the romance of the Canaveral National Seashore

The Canaveral National Seashore includes close to 58,000 acres of lagoon, barrier islands, pine flatwoods, offshore waters, and more. It's massive and it's gorgeous. It also includes 24 miles of stunning beach and is the home of thousands of protected and endangered animals. You and your special someone are sure to run into some marine turtles there should you spend some time exploring this stunning beach and shoreline. This is another fantastic spot for a relaxing picnic; or perhaps you might want to set up for a pristine sunrise photo shoot. This seashore screams romance and comes highly recommended for those looking for an outdoor excursion along the eastern coast.

🌐 www.nps.gov/CANA

f www.facebook.com/CanaveralNatlSeashore

📍 212 S Washington Ave. Titusville, FL 327960

33

Enjoy the elegance of the Hollis Garden

At the Hollis Garden, architecture meets nature in a dazzling display of class and style to create a stunning visual experience. There, you will find gorgeous, sprawling flowerbeds, ornamental fountains and some extremely interesting works of public art. They boast a collection of more than 10,000 flowers, native trees and ornamental shrubs, so you will have plenty to see should you find yourself there. The 1.2-acre locale is nestled neatly within Lake Mirror Park and the entire experience from top to bottom is equal parts romantic and serene. This is another wonderful place to take a nice stroll either before or after a meal. We highly recommend this destination should you be staying anywhere between Tampa and Orlando.

📍 702 E Orange St, Lakeland, FL 33801

Admire the elegance of the Albin Polasek Museum & Sculpture Gardens

Since 1961, the Albin Polasek Museum & Sculpture Gardens has astonished visitors with unparalleled elegance and beauty. There are more than 200 creations from the Czech-born Polasek, and each one is breathtaking in its own right. There are guided tours to enjoy, a chapel and residence to explore, and of course, an outdoor sculpture garden that is unlike anything you will ever see. The museum itself is listed on the National Register of Historic Places; the artwork and history there are an integral part of the fabric of the nation. Simply put, it is impossible to walk the grounds without feeling invigorated and full of life. This is a wonderful place to take your travel companion and recharge your emotional batteries.

🌐 polasek.org

f www.facebook.com/PolasekMuseum

📍 633 Osceola Ave., Winter Park, FL 32789

35

See the art of the world at the Leepa-Rattner Museum of Art

The Leepa-Rattner Museum of Art offers a little taste of everything; there you will find history, culture, education and more. This sophisticated destination is the perfect spot to reinvigorate your senses and reawaken your imagination together with your loved one. The Leepa-Rattner Museum of Art has been open for nearly two decades, and it offers modern art spanning the 20th and 21st centuries. Its more than 6,000 pieces of artwork will offer plenty for you to peruse with your most special someone. The museum is part of the Tarpon Springs Campus of St. Petersburg College, and the thorough dedication to education is obvious. There is so much incredible culture in beautiful Tarpon Springs, and you will be certain to find the best of it at the Leepa-Rattner Museum of Art.

🌐 www.leeparattner.org

f www.facebook.com/leeparattner

📍 600 E Klosterman Rd Tarpon Springs, FL 34689

36

Seek tranquility at Wat Mongkolratanaram

If you're in Tampa looking for a place to decompress, find your inner peace, and potentially see something brand new, visit the Wat Tampa Buddhist temple. The temple itself is 35-feet high and architecturally beautiful in its own right. The overwhelming feeling of calmness surrounding it is, quite literally, divine and you will not regret immersing yourself in its understated but exquisitely artistic presence. This is a great place to visit regardless of your cultural background and a great way to downshift from an aggressive vacation schedule. We highly suggest a peaceful meditation in the garden by Palm River, too. There, you will find the perfect place to practice your "Dharma." Give Wat Mongkolratanaram a try, and be overcome with joyful relaxation!

wattampainenglish.com

www.facebook.com/pages/Wat%20Mongkolratanaram%20Buddhist%20Temple/102381826513249

5306 Palm River Rd Tampa, FL, US 33619

37

Enjoy the history of Heritage Village

Heritage Village is a one-of-a-kind hamlet that will give any Florida visitor a broad taste of the rich history of beautiful Pinellas County. With exhibits, programs, and an impressive collection of historical items to see and experience, Heritage Village is a great place to soak in some sun and stroll about, all while taking in some great local history while you visit. At Heritage Village, you will find everything from a sugar cane mill to an old church, a windmill, water tower, and even their own House of Seven Gables. Hand-in-hand with your best guy or gal, Heritage Village is a wonderful way to bring some educational tranquility to any Florida vacation.

---

www.pinellascounty.org/Heritage

www.facebook.com/PinellasCountyNews

11909 125th St, Largo, FL 33774

38

Build memories at the Pier 60 Sugar Sand Festival

If you are looking for a cool way to enjoy Clearwater Beach, give the Pier 60 Sugar Sand Festival a gander. One of the absolute best sand-sculpting festivals in the state, it showcases the work of world-recognized sand artists competing against each other to make the most spectacular natural sculptures in the Sunshine State. At Pier 60, you'll find 1,000 tons of sand "sand-crafted" in a 21,000 sq. ft. building to create an incredible walkthrough experience that you won't forget. There is also fireworks, music and sculpting classes for those looking for something a little extra at Pier 60, too!

———————————

🌐 www.sugarsandfestival.com

f www.facebook.com/Pier60SugarSandFestival

📍 1 Causeway Blvd, Clearwater Beach, FL 33767

39

Marvel at the Wizarding World of Harry Potter

This is the premier Harry Potter experience, where you will feel like you will be able to cast your own "patronus" charm by the time you finish up a day of exploring there. There, you can hang out in Diagon Alley, skulk around beneath the notorious Gringotts bank, and even visit the famed wizard village of Hogsmeade. Of course, you will also be able to see the magnificent, legendary Hogwarts Castle with some of the most state-of-the-art entertainment attraction technology in the world. This is the spot for any movie buff, fantasy enthusiast, or really, anyone who has a pulse at all! Enjoy the rides, shows, dining and more at this spell-tacular part of the Universal Orlando Resort.

🌐 www.universalorlando.com/web/en/us/universal-orlando-resort

f www.facebook.com/UniversalOrlandoResort

📍 6000 Universal Blvd., Orlando, FL 32819

Take to the skies with Florida Air Tours

Who doesn't want to see Florida from the sky? The state has such a variety of ecosystems, natural sights, and spectacular constructions that to get a real sense of what the state offers, you just have to head into the open blue skies. Florida Air Tours provides both Biplane Tours and Helicopter Tours you can enjoy with your sweetheart. Experience the wonderful feeling of soaring through the clear Florida skies while taking in the sights from the front seat of a vintage WWII-era biplane. Or, view the incredible sights of Florida's coastlines and classic landmarks from the perspective of a Robinson R-44 helicopter.

🌐 www.floridaairtours.com

f www.facebook.com/FloridaAirTours

📍 475 Manor Dr Merritt Island, FL 32952

41

X marks the spot at Treasure Island Beach

Let the cool ocean breeze bathe over you as you stroll along the St. Petersburg Municipal Beach at Treasure Island, one the city's most magnificent hidden jewels. The warm sand, shining sun and sounds of the crashing waves are the perfect setting for a romantic picnic or long walk along the coast with your partner. This gorgeous beach has volleyball, snacks, ample public access and much more. You could spend the whole day relaxing along the water; or maybe you'd like to take an after-dinner stroll to watch the sunset. No matter how you slice it, a visit to the St. Petersburg Municipal Beach at Treasure Island will hit you just right regardless of how you decide to spend your time there.

🌐 www.stpeteparksrec.org/treasureisland

f www.facebook.com/stpeteparksrec

📍 11260 Gulf Blvd. St. Petersburg, FL 33706

42

See the unbelievable Treasure Island Slide

The slippery Treasure Island Hippo slide is massive, and after you brave it once you will definitely want to go down over and over again. Its proprietors boast that it's the world's tallest inflatable slide, at a full four stories high! You have got to see this thing to believe it. You and your partner are definitely going to need to bring your nerves of steel for a ride down the world-renowned Hippo. For those brave enough, this is a fun way to get wet, cool off from the hot Florida sun, and feel like a kid all over again. Not for the faint of heart, but definitely a worthwhile experience for you thrill seekers out there. The Treasure Island slides are straight up (or down!) boatloads of fun!

🌐 www.bigeventslides.com

ⓕ www.facebook.com/TreasureIslandSlide

📍 10400 Gulf Blvd., Treasure Island, FL 33706

43

Admire the beauty of the Weedon Island Preserve

This expansive preserve offers up more than 3,000 acres of gorgeous nature, including a coastal system with both upland and aquatic ecosystems. There, you will see countless animals and native plants, and it has some of the best fishing and bird watching in all of the greater Tampa Bay region. You can also visit Weedon Island Preserve's educational facility and learn about the cultural history and the indigenous peoples who inhabited the land for centuries. A trip to Weedon Island is equal parts science, history and welcome tranquility. Bring a camera, bring your binoculars, and see what you can spot. There are so many different things to see, you are going to need to record them all!

🌐 www.weedonislandpreserve.org

ⓕ www.facebook.com/WeedonIslandPreserve

📍 1800 Weedon Drive NE, St. Petersburg, FL 33702

Delight in the beauty of Palmer Orchids

At Palmer Orchids you will find some of the most beautiful flowers in central Florida; you will also find everything you need to cultivate and grow you own resplendent orchid garden. Stop in and browse these diverse and spectacular floral displays with your best guy or gal for a truly wonderful visual treat. Of course, you can order flowers from them ahead of time as well, but the nursery is a sight to behold. While you are there, you may even run into some local gardening societies or orchid clubs; this is the perfect place to learn everything you need to know about these beautiful flowers, and maybe even pick one up for your special someone!

🌐 www.palmerorchids.com

f www.facebook.com/palmerorchidsnursery

📍 22700 Taylor Dr., Bradenton, FL 34211

45

Look to the sky at the Sarasota Audubon Nature Center

When you are at the Sarasota Audubon Nature Center, look up! There you will find some of the most beautiful birds in Florida singing, chirping and fluttering about at this top-flight nature center. The center offers everything from nature walks to park cleanups to speakers, and local and even international trips. Nature lovers will adore this place, but so too will anyone looking for something you can scarcely find outside of Sarasota. The signature project of the nature center is a Beach Nesting Bird Program where volunteers work toward the conservation of Least Terns, Black Skimmers and Snowy Plovers, who are trying to navigate the myriad challenges of beach life. Give the Sarasota Audubon Nature Center a chance to lift you and your special someone off your feet.

www.sarasotaaudubon.org

www.facebook.com/SarasotaAudubonSociety

999 Center Road, Sarasota, FL 34240

Dive in to the Mote Marine Laboratory & Aquarium

There are few places more beautiful and exotic than the sea, and at the Mote Marine Laboratory & Aquarium, you'll see all manner of underwater wonders and creatures that truly showcase the wonder and majesty of the open ocean. Focused on science, research, exploration and education, this is a wonderful place to come learn about the mysterious depths of the ocean and the creatures that inhabit them. Incredibly, this place grew from a mere one-room laboratory into a formidable institution of research and conservation that you will not want to skip. Among some of the amazing creatures you will learn about there are sharks, sea turtles, dolphins, manatees and even coral reefs. They say the ocean is their passion—it will be yours as well, should you find yourself visiting them in sunny Sarasota during your Florida vacation.

🌐 www.mote.org

f www.facebook.com/MoteMarineLab

📍 1600 Ken Thompson Parkway, Sarasota, FL 34236

47

Stroll the boardwalk at Pier 60 Clearwater

Pier 60 Clearwater is a 1,080-foot fishing pier and recreational park that you can meander down at any time of the day. The pier itself stretches out into the clear waters, a sturdy wooden bridge to the ocean, offering remarkable views during the day and dazzling sunsets over the ocean at night. offers a complete line of fishing tackle, t-shirts, souvenirs, and more, whether you plan to go fishing or want to watch the professionals bring in their catches. The most common fish you'll find off the pier include the Spanish mackerel, spotted and silver trout, redfish, tarpon, and flounder. There is also a beautiful view of the sunset that's so magnificent, there's a festival each and every night to celebrate it, with music, entertainers, and art vendors, all sharing a memorable experience under the spectacular crimson light of the setting sun over the ocean. It's the perfect way to end your day, any day of the week!

🌐 www.visitstpeteclearwater.com/profile/pier-60-clearwater-beach/1570

f www.facebook.com/Pier60ClearwaterBeachFlorida

📍 1 Causeway Blvd Clearwater, FL 33767

Scare yourselves at Sir Henry's Haunted Trail

You'd best be snuggled up closely to your travel partner if you decide to hit up Sir Henry's Haunted Trail; it is an absolutely frightening experience from top to bottom! This outdoor attraction comes with terrifying trails to explore, laser tag, and an escape game in addition to live entertainment. Located between Tampa and Orlando, this is another great spot for those Florida travelers hanging out in the heart of the state, and it is definitely a must-see if you are vacationing around Halloween time. Sir Henry is still looking for the killer of his beloved bride; see if you can help him out should you be in the neighborhood!

🌐 www.sirhenryshauntedtrail.com

f www.facebook.com/sirhenryshauntedtrail

📍 2837 South Frontage Rd. Plant City, FL 33566

49

Go where the Magic Kingdom meets the Animal Kingdom

The Magic of Disney meets the majesty of the wild at this first-class tourist destination. Kilimanjaro, Everest and the Kali River are all just a short trot from one another at this magnificent home to animals from all over the world. Hear the lions roar, watch the tigers stalk and enjoy some of the most exciting them park rides on the planet. Naturally, you will want to budget at least a whole day at this park; its quite large geographically and it can be pretty grueling to hit all the notables in one shot. Should you have a chance to visit—the accompanying hotel is also quite spectacular—you will be in for a once-in-a-lifetime vacation experience.

🌐 disneyworld.disney.go.com/destinations/animal-kingdom

f www.facebook.com/WaltDisneyWorld

📍 2901 Osceola Pkwy, Bay Lake, FL 34747

Visit the opulent mansion of a Ringling Brother

Formerly the home of John Ringling, of the Ringling Brothers Circus, and his wife Mable, the Ca'd'Zan Mansion is one of the most eccentric mansions in all of the United States. With an astonishing price tag of $1.5 million when construction began in 1924, after John died, the mansion was bequeathed to the state of Florida. It's a stellar building of pale beige stone, elegantly highlighted by dazzling brickwork, swooping, airy terracotta roofs, and gothic-inspired carved windows. Due to the costs of maintaining it, the mansion was used in 1996 for the Hollywood remake of "Great Expectations" due to the rundown condition. Revived by the state in 2002 and opened to the general public, you and your partner can take a tour of the residence and get a glimpse into the opulent private lives of the Ringlings.

🌐 www.ringling.org/ca-dzan

ⓕ www.facebook.com/pages/Ca-dZan/120304718016068

📍 Sarasota, FL 34243

CHAPTER TWO
11 Ideas to Hear in Central Florida

Whether it's a night of smooth jazz or a head-banging concert in one of Central Florida's innumerable venues, there's plenty for a couple to go hear in this region of the state. Check out our listings for the best things for a couple to hear, and go share a memorable experience with your loved one!

01

Feel the beat with RythmTrail Steel Drum Band

This Caribbean steel drum band boasts an impressive schedule that includes more than 300 shows played each year. Simply put, they are one of the most highly sought-after bands in the state as they delight listeners with smooth jams, neat beats, and a wide array of music to choose from. They can deliver festive on the dime, or if you are so inclined, they can also play something a little more romantic to set the mood for you and your significant other. While they're regular performers in Jacksonville, Miami and Tampa, they also play all over the state and the country. This is a really cool band and we highly recommend giving them a try if you're looking for the rhythm of the islands.

🌐 www.rythmtrail.com

f www.facebook.com/Rythmtrailsteeldrumband

📍 3200 N Hiawassee Rd., FL 32818

Get down with the Orlando DJ Group

The Orlando DJ Group is comprised of true entertainment experts. Since 2007, they have kept central Florida dancing, moving and grooving everywhere from bars to weddings, restaurants and corporate events. They are pro-grade, they are fun to watch, and they have boatloads of experience to handle whatever situation you need them for. The Orlando DJ Group also has the best gear in the business, and they will deliver on whatever it is you are looking for. Simply stated, these guys are great at their jobs, and you are going to want to give them a go should you need to jam out in the greater Orlando area.

🌐 www.orlandodjgroup.com

f www.facebook.com/OrlandoDJGroup

📍 Orlando DJ Group, 4202 Ilene Ct., Orlando, FL 32806

03

Catch some tunes at the Hideaway Café

The Hideaway Café is part recording studio, part performance venue, and part restaurant. This is a one-of-a-kind place that blends the best elements of music, entertainment and delicious food. There are not a lot of places around where you can watch real musicians actually record their tunes, so this is definitely something you will want to try—especially if you are a true music lover—if you are staying anywhere near St. Petersburg during your travels. And don't underestimate the menu, either! Everything about the Hideaway Café is done with soul and flair, including the food; so grab your duet partner and give it a chance during your Florida excursion.

🌐 www.hideawaycafe.biz

f www.facebook.com/hideawayCafe

📍 1756 Central Ave., St. Petersburg, FL 33712

Let the Sarasota Orchestra sweep you off your feet

The Sarasota Orchestra is extremely talented, and their musical stylings evoke just about every emotional response you can think of. From their Classics Concerts to their "Pops" series at Holley Hall, they have something for music fans of every type. Having a night out at the orchestra is one of the most inherently romantic things you can do. The strings' melodies and the woodwinds' captivating tones will surely move you and your travel companion every which way. There are lots of things to do at night in central Florida, but be sure to mix in some romance and intrigue alongside the raucous club and bar scene. You will be glad you did, especially after a night with the Sarasota Orchestra.

---

www.sarasotaorchestra.org

www.facebook.com/Sarasotaorchestra

709 N Tamiami Tr, Sarasota, FL 34236

05

Laugh yourself silly at the SAK Comedy Lab

One of the best date nights imaginable in the state of Florida is taking your sweetheart to the SAK Comedy Lab. Since 1991, the professional ensemble of improv actors has entertained audiences with a brand of live, improvised comedy. The performers take in suggestions from the audience, make up characters, and create songs right on the spot. This is an attraction that's all about performers entertaining with words and music. With an edgy appeal that makes this a fun, adult-only activity, it's an attraction where you'll be surrounded by delightful comedy from the stage and laughter from the audience.

🌐 www.sakcomedylab.com

ⓕ www.facebook.com/sakcomedylab

📍 29 S Orange Ave Orlando, FL 32801

Chill out at the Lakeland Loft

As a cigar lounge, jazz club, and bar all rolled into one, this vintage, smooth-feeling jazz & blues spot is going to totally whisk you away from your everyday stresses. Hear the classics and new smooth jazz creations fill the ultra-premium upscale lounge, located in the beautiful and historic town of Lakeland; enjoy over 4,000-square-feet of Oxford-style décor and crystal chandeliers that will make you feel like you're stepping back in time. Sit back and enjoy one of these local performances that you will never forget.

www.lakelandloft.com

www.facebook.com/LakelandLoft

108 S Tennessee Ave Lakeland, FL 33801

07

Enjoy a concert at the Daytona Beach Bandshell

After a day of exploring and nourishing, why not unwind with a free concert at the Daytona Beach Bandshell? There is not much that is better than music on the beach, which is why this concert venue will have you and your partner smiling in awe as the sun sets in the distance. Designed to provide optimal acoustics for the many musical acts that have shared the stage over the years, this bandshell has attracted some seriously famous performers, including the likes of Elton John, Journey, Santana, Van Halen, and more. Be sure to check the schedule ahead of time, as there is not live music available every single day. With a little luck and planning, you might find one of your favorite groups or singers providing an unforgettable beachside concert experience.

🌐 www.daytonabeach.com/events/festivals-and-music/band-shell-concerts

ⓕ www.facebook.com/daytonabeachbandshell

📍 70 Boardwalk Daytona Beach, FL 32118

Listen to waterfalls at the Sunken Gardens

Back with another garden recommendation, the Sunken Gardens in St. Petersburg, Florida, are packed with hidden paths, stunning exotic plants, and tons of sparkling waterfalls you'll be able to hear from any place in the park. There's nothing like the quiet, perpetual roar of a waterfall, tons of water pounding the rocky base over the cliffs. Often you can hear them before you see them, and once you do, you'll never forget it. If you sit back, close your eyes, and allow your ears to do the exploring, you'll feel drawn away into a tropical paradise that will place your mind at ease. You can also check out the spectacular living museum and some of the oldest living tropical plants in the area.

🌐 www.visitstpeteclearwater.com/profile/sunken-gardens/1979

f www.facebook.com/SunkenGardens

📍 1825 4th St N, St. Petersburg, FL 33704

---- **09** ----

Enjoy old-fashioned opulence at the Tampa Theatre

The refurbished and revived historical theatre is one of the last great 1920 theatre palaces in Floridian Greco-Spanish-Persian architecture still around today. With a ceiling painted to resemble a night sky with twinkling stars, adorned with gargoyles, Greek statues, and other Mediterranean accents that will have you wondering if you're in Spain or Florida, the Tampa Theatre is even home to vaudeville-era dressing rooms, plus an original Wurlitzer Theatre Organ. During the mid-20th century, the theatre underwent a revival and was listed on the National Register of Historic Places in 1978. Its unique acoustics make every show a delight enhanced by its surroundings. Today, you can enjoy a variety of performances, shows, music displays, and plays put on by the nonprofit company that manages the theatre.

🌐 www.tampatheatre.org

f www.facebook.com/TampaTheatre

📍 711 N Franklin St Tampa, FL 33602

Hear magnificent singing at Sarasota Opera

If you want to sit down and see a proper opera put on by Florida's finest, then it's time to make your way over to the Sarasota Opera. You'll hear classically trained singers send notes soaring to the heavens as they bring to life operas which have been delighting music lovers for decades or even centuries. The venue produces outstanding opera true to vision of the composer to entertain, enrich, and educate the surrounding community, as well as visitors from around the world. The venue is available for America-trained principal artists, on a mission to increase the visibility of opera in the 21st century. If you haven't been to a show there yet, be sure to add it to your list.

🌐 www.sarasotaopera.org

f www.facebook.com/sarasotaopera

📍 61 N Pineapple Ave Sarasota, FL 34236

11

Groove to the classics with the Matt Winter Band

Have Matt delight your ears by himself or let the whole nine-musician set really bring the noise home. This band offers an enormous setlist and has a huge array of musical stylings to choose from. They cover everything from the pop hits, to throwbacks, classic rock, country music, funk, R&B and more, and they do it all with style and class. This is one of the greater Tampa Bay area's best acts and they come with equal parts energy and musicianship. Let the Matt Winter Band take care of all your musical needs and give them a shot should you feel the need to cut loose and break out your dancing shoes. They rock hard!

———————————————

🌐 www.mattwinterband.com

f www.facebook.com/mattwinterband

CHAPTER THREE
69 Ideas to Taste in Central Florida

T here's no shortage of marvelous restaurants in this vacation state, where the best culinary traditions from the Caribbean and beyond blend with American ingenuity and passion to create memorable dining experiences. Whether you and your date are looking for a fancy night on the town, or just a bite on the road in Central Florida, we've got you covered!

01

Enjoy the cuisine of Africa at Selam Ethiopian & Eritrean Cuisine

Known for a blend of spices color, and a burst of flavor, Selam Ethiopian & Eritrean Cuisine provides authentic African culinary immersion right from the state of Florida. Seasoned lentils and sizzling meats, served on the tangy, sour fermented flatbread that is the traditional Ethiopian plate, taste the true pageantry of Ethiopian food, both from a sit-down setting, as well as takeout. Located centrally in Orlando, Florida, the restaurant is a cornerstone in the local community, having been recognized for excellent service and friendly staff. This unique dining place is a romantic setting for you and your significant other.

www.ethiopianrestaurantorlando.com

www.facebook.com/selamethiopiancousine

5494 Central Florida Parkway Orlando, FL, US 32821

Enjoy down-home specialties at Oakwood Smokehouse

This growing restaurant company established in 1998 in Lake County Florida, Oakwood Smokehouse is a full-service casual restaurant staffed by professional managers for a total luxury experience. Enjoy specialty salads and Oakwood smoked barbecue, as well as charbroiled burgers, center cut steaks, grilled chicken, fresh soups, and of course, their famed ribs. For those feeling like some seafood, they have a delicious Mahi Mahi sandwich, and it's all available with their signature fried okra and collard greens – a Southern staple. Plus, with an open kitchen design, eating at Oakwood Smokehouse offers more than smoky flavors – they offer ambience, too. Enjoy the delicious simplicity of this cozy dining location.

www.oakwoodsmokehouse.com/site

www.facebook.com/Oakwood-Smokehouse-107667647600550

860 US-441, Lady Lake, FL 32159

03

Get authentic at Sandra's German Restaurant

You might not be able to pronounce all the menu items at Sandra's German Restaurant, but that should not stop you from ordering them; they are both delicious and filling. Try the Leberknoedel Suppe (liver dumpling soup) or the Schweinsbraten (Bavarian roast pork) for a truly authentic taste of German cuisine located conveniently in beautiful Saint Pete Beach. Of course, the brats and schnitzel are on the money as well, but if you are looking for some unique offerings that you might not be able to get at other Euro-centric restaurants, give those tongue twisters a try. The restaurant itself is delightful and lively and we highly recommend both the area and this German eatery.

www.sandrasgermanrestaurantstpetebeach.com

www.facebook.com/Sandrasgermanrestaurant

7115 Gulf Blvd., Saint Pete Beach, FL 33706

Raise a glass at Intracoastal Brewing Company

The Intracoastal Brewing Company is located smack dab in the middle of the Eau Gallie Arts District and has been handling the needs of thirsty drinkers in Melbourne and on the Atlantic coast for years. The brewing company boasts an impressive list of seasonally rotating recipes, and the expert staff there will point you in the right direction for whatever you happen to be craving. Hit up the Intracoastal Brewing Company after enjoying some of the finest entertainment the "Space Coast" has to offer; the brews are great, and you will feel right at home amongst the warm bartending staff.

intracoastalbrewingcompany.com/news

www.facebook.com/intracoastalbrewingcompany

652 West Eau Gallie Blvd, Melbourne, FL 32935

05

Taste the freshness at Sushi Ushi Japanese Restaurant

Known for their modern takes on traditional classics, Sushi Ushi has some of Valrico's best eat-in and takeout sushi menu options. They boast great service, creative menu items, and an authentic experience for all their guests. They use only the best-quality ingredients, and it shows in their work. If you are a seafood or sushi lover, you will definitely appreciate the care they put into their rolls. If you are a newcomer, give them a chance to make you a believer. The menu is substantial, and they also offer hibachi. We highly recommend giving them a try if you are in the mood for some of the freshest seafood in town!

www.sushiushivalrico.com

www.facebook.com/sushiushivalrico

1713 State Rd 60 E, Valrico, FL 33594

Set a spell at Southern Harmony Cafe

Due west of Orlando is all-too-often under-appreciated Ridge Manor, Florida. There, you will find a very charming, quaint café serving up southern home-cooked meals that you will absolutely adore. The Southern Harmony Cafe offers a range of Cajun foods and other Southern favorites for breakfast and brunch that will make you feel like you are back eating at grandma's countertop. The team at the Southern Harmony Café is warm and welcoming, the café is cozy, and the quiet seclusion of the area really creates a wonderful experience for those staying in the area or passing through on the way to the Tampa Bay region. Come back again and again, too, as they always have something new and exciting to try!

---

www.facebook.com/southernharmonycafe

34508 Cortez Blvd, Ridge Manor, FL 33523

07

Drink up at GB Bottle Shop & Tasting Bar

GB's Bottle Shop and Tasting Bar is the perfect partner to south Orlando's The Gnarly Barley. In fact, they go together almost as good as you and your traveling companion (almost)! This location offers some of the finest craft beer in the region and some really nice wines to pair with any meal or occasion. They will also let you drink while you browse, so you and your partner can relax a little while you decide on what you might want to bring home. They cater to both the casual drinker and the hardcore afficionado, so whatever your level of interest is they will have something for you. For a nice time taking in some of central Florida's best brews, give GB Bottle Shop and Tasting Bar a try.

🌐 www.gbbottleshop.com

📘 www.facebook.com/gbbottleshop

📍 531 Virginia Dr, Orlando, FL 32803

08

Brilliant Private Chef

If you are looking for a fun activity for you and your travel partner, try cooking dinner together under the guidance of the Sunshine State's very own Brilliant Private Chef. Offering cooking classes, events, parties and, naturally, romantic dinners for two, this is a fun, interactive way to enjoy a homecooked meal on vacation. There are, of course, lots of great restaurants and eateries to choose from while touring the state, but don't forget the value of rolling up your sleeves, chopping and slicing some fresh foods, and putting together a masterpiece of your own for you and your partner. Plan ahead for this one, too, and be sure you are ready to put a personal touch into your romantic vacation dinner!

---

www.facebook.com/Evasnaturalcuisine

09

Go Mediterranean at Mio's Grill & Cafe

The culture and diversity of restaurant offerings in central Florida is laudable, and one of the many great things about that diversity is the tremendous Mediterranean food options travelers have to choose from when visiting there. Mio's Grill & Café in St. Petersburg is a perfect example of such; they have a beautiful blend of Turkish and Greek menu items that will not disappoint a hungry couple. The portions are sizable and the prices are affordable. We loved Mio's for the flavors, the fun and their commitment to bringing the Mediterranean Sea to the beautiful west coast of Florida. This is great spot for a fun night laughing over a big, fat beef gyro platter.

🌐 miosgrill.com

f www.facebook.com/miosgrill

📍 119 2nd St N, St. Petersburg, FL 33701

Experience fine Asian dining at Maihana

Located inside of Kobe Japanese Steakhouses International Drive and Lake Buena Vista is the Maihana Asian Cuisine: an upscale dining experience. Sink your teeth into the crispy Peking Duck Lettuce Wrap appetizer and a Scorpion Bowl cocktail, a powerful concoction of rums and other spirits laced with orange zest. If that doesn't tickle your fancy, consider the Curry Lamb Chops, Miso Sea Bass, Black Bean Scallops, and other savory seafood delicacies you're going to adore. The Orlando-based restaurant is laid-back, high quality, and a perfect destination for a surprise date night.

———————————————

🌐 www.maihana.com

f www.facebook.com/MaihanaIDR

📍 8148 International Drive Orlando, FL 32819

11

Have a slice at J. J. Gandy's Pies, Inc.

Cheese pie, cream pie, key lime pie, and more are all on the table at J. J. Gandy's Pies, Inc. This operation is built on customer service, appreciation, and care as they work hard every day to deliver the finest specialty pies in Palm Harbor. Should you be visiting during the fall or winter, their Pumpkin Chiffon pie is an absolute delight. Be warned, though, you may want to order ahead as Gandy's churns out pies by the thousands during the holidays! Don't forget, too, they have some great breads, cookies, brownies and other treats to choose from, if you are not a pie person. Bring your special someone here and grab something sweet; everyone wins with a trip to J.J Gandy's Pies, Inc.

🌐 www.jjgandys.com

f www.facebook.com/JJ-Gandys-Pies-116224241734892

📍 3725 Alt 19, Palm Harbor, FL 34683

Taste Colombian Flavors at Que-Rico

For a little taste of Columbia south of Venice, this is the place to hit. The Chicken Stew is a signature meal and the Mojarra Frita is both exotic and delicious. This food really sizzles! They are located just a stone's throw from Highland Ridge Park on the Tamiami Trail in North Port, so this is a great spot to settle into after a day exploring south-central Florida. One of the best things about the Florida dining scene is how well they do international food, and Que-Rico Colombian Flavors is a prime example of that reality. Hit them up for a delicious and authentic taste of South America you will not want to forget!

www.orderquericocolombianflavors.com

www.facebook.com/QueRicoFlavors

30 S 13648 Tamiami Tr., North Port, FL 34287

13

Find delight at Crepe Delicious

Like the name suggests, the crepes there are most certainly delicious, but they are also incredibly healthy, too. A point of pride for the international chain, they offer both savory and sweet crepes with an emphasis on using healthy ingredients. Buckwheat, rice and wheat are among some of the bases they use in these tasty breakfast treats, and all of them are made fresh to order with a miniscule 170 calories and only three grams of fat. This is also a great stop if you are looking for a meal on the go, so keep that in mind as you plot your Florida adventure. There is a seemingly endless list of things you can have in your crepe, so start thinking about what you are going to fill yours with now!

🌐 www.crepedelicious.com

📘 www.facebook.com/CrepeDelicious

📍 55 W Church St., Orlando, FL 32801

Experience Cremesh European Restaurant

Chef Pavel treats cooking like part art form and part music making as he brings some of the best flavors Europe has to offer to Bradenton. Among their many offerings are pork shank, beef goulash, wiener schnitzel, and all sorts of delectable seafood to choose from. The menu covers much of the continent, so no matter what tickles you fancy, there is sure to be something there to satisfy your tastebuds. And, once you are finished with your meal, you can top it all off with the chef's specialty "Cremesh"—an incredible after-dinner treat featuring vanilla custard, seasonal fruit, and puff pastry. You will be stuffed to the brim with the enchanting treats of continents afar after a night at Cremesh European Restaurant!

cremeshrestaurant.com

www.facebook.com/Cremeshrestaurant

7232 Manatee Avenue West, Bradenton, FL 34209

15

Alsace French Bistro

It should be no surprise that the French onion soup at the Alsace French Bistro is magnificent; they have one of the best selections of French cuisine you will find in all of Florida. They also have an exceptional crispy duck entrée, diced chicken breast and a classic beef stew cooked with red wine, carrots, onions and even bacon! This is what French food is supposed to taste like! The atmosphere is as romantic as the country itself and the service is nothing short of exceptional. This remote little stretch of peninsula is the perfect setting for a sunset and night out to dinner in the greater Tampa Bay region.

🌐 alsace.french.bistro.free.fr/index.html

f www.facebook.com/Alsace-french-bistro-1283642728411339

📍 1120 pinellas bayway south apt#114 Tierra Verde, FL 33715

16

Taste the happiness at Fresh Kitchen

The folks at Fresh Kitchen believe preparing and eating food ought to be done the right way; healthily, tastily and aimed at energizing and nourishing those who consumer it. Simply stated, food and happiness go hand-in-hand and Fresh Kitchen is dedicated to that marriage. At Fresh Kitchen, you can re-energize with their delicious, pressed juices, frescas, teas and more. They also offer seasonal menus that rotate with available ingredients. The meats at Fresh Kitchen are always seared to perfection, and the noodles, rice, veggies and quinoa will have you feeling like a million bucks. Stop in to recharge as you are biking, hiking and exploring everything central Florida has to offer. You (and your body) will be glad you did!

🌐 www.eatfreshkitchen.com

f www.facebook.com/eatfk

📍 851 N. Alafaya Trail Q01, Orlando, FL 32828

17

Experience the exotic at Susuru

This place screams style. With its awesome wood paneling covered in Chinese signs, cool hanging fixtures, and warm lighting, you will be blown away by the attention to detail they put into creating the Susuru experience. The menu is compact, but the proprietors there are clearly focused on quality over quantity. This is also a great place to get a drink and try some far-eastern libations you might not be able to get at your run-of-the-mill bar. The drink menu is bursting with exotic flavors that will keep you on your toes all night and the diversity of the drinks is truly something special. This is a wonderful date night locale that mixes in wild flavors and an exceptional atmosphere.

🌐 www.susuruorl.com

f www.facebook.com/susuruorl

📍 Susuru, 8548 Palm Pkwy, Orlando, FL 32836

Authentic Sulphur Taste of Chengdu

This place is so authentic the menu is written in another language! We may not be able to read it, but we sure do think it tastes pretty amazing. They make a fantastic Kungpao Chicken with onions and peanuts that is drizzled in a delectable spicy sauce. In fact, every time they drizzle anything, they really hit their mark. The team at the Sulphur Taste of Chengdu says that their goal is to explore the traditions of Sichuan cuisine as they play off the fragrant, fresh and spicy flavors it is known for; we are not going to argue with them! We loved everything about this place, including the outstanding staff and friendly service.

---

www.facebook.com/tasteofchengdu

2030 West Colonial Drive Orlando, FL, US 32804

19

Bite into a burger at Thee Burger Spot

The top spot for a burger is, you guessed it, Thee Burger Spot! This family-owned establishment is proud to serve Tampa residents from families to football stars, and they all show up in droves for good reason. The food there is really, really good! The burgers are juicy, stuffed to the max, and cooked exactly the way you like; what's more, they come with the finest golden fries in town. Naturally, they have other options for the less-beef inclined, but if you are craving a juicy burger after a day of swimming you are going to want to be at Thee Burger Spot. Also, don't forget to top it all off with Augustine's Cheesecake: a heavenly combination of salted caramel, banana pudding and red velvet.

www.theeburgerspot.com

www.facebook.com/theeburgerspottampa813

3917 N. Tampa St., Tampa, FL 33603

Experience the Lechonera Merengue

Lechonera Merengue brings "grandma style Dominican goodness," as they say, to every meal and you are going to feel their passion for cooking in each and every dish they serve up. They are known for their "Sancocho," but pretty much everything on the menu is absolutely delicious. As charming and adorable as Kissimmee itself, Lechonera Merengue checks all the boxes for a great vacation eatery: exotic flavors, great staff, and an awesome location. We highly recommend this spot for those staying in and around Osceola County looking for a taste of the Dominican Republic. We have no doubt you will leave happy and satisfied.

---

 www.facebook.com/lechoneramerengue

 3260 Vineland Rd. Suite 101A, Kissimmee, FL 34746

21

Eastern European flair at Salt & Sweet Restaurant

This is the way to go for traditional Polish cuisine if you are spending your vacation time in central Florida. This place is absolutely gorgeous top to bottom, and it sets the mood nicely for a quiet evening out with your travel companion. This Melbourne destination hits all the right notes with its traditional Polish offerings, including pierogis, sausage, and a "Zrazy Polskie" that brilliantly blends beef, sautéed onions, pickles, peppers, red cabbage, and more. The food there is good, the service there is good, and you will love the ambiance. They also have a nice selection of wine and beer, so if you are in the mood for a little eastern European libation during your date night, we highly recommend the Salt & Sweet Restaurant.

🌐 www.saltandsweet.net

📍 3092 Lake Washington Rd., Melbourne, FL 32934

Go green at the Claddagh Cottage Irish Pub

At the Claddagh Cottage Irish Pub you will be served a "proper" pint of Guinness, fantastic home-style Irish cuisine and sit in an atmosphere reminiscent of the Emerald Isle itself. This newly updated building is the perfect location for a pub, and we can all but guarantee you won't leave hungry or thirsty after a night out there. Another great thing about the Claddagh Cottage Irish Pub is the live music; on select nights you will be treated to traditional Irish tunes while you eat and drink your night away. They have pros, they have amateurs, and they have fun! Stop in for a real-deal overseas culinary experience; your travel partner will be "lucky" to spend an evening there with you!

🌐 claddaghcottagepub.com

f www.facebook.com/CladdaghCottagePub

📍 2421 Curry Ford Rd, Orlando, FL 32806

23

Try the biggest cookie you've ever seen at Gideon's Bakehouse Bakery

If you're looking for a big-time cookie delight, then head over to Gideon's Bakery where you can enjoy two-pound cookies. The cookies are so big and delicious that they bakery comes with a 6-cookie per person limit in the store. Enormous, fragrant, and deliciously browned, it takes a special skill for their bakers to produce these giant and unusual delights. With all goodies being 100% handmade so they can control the quality and ingredients, the bakery only offers in-person visits, which means it's time for you to go check it out in Orlando, Florida. Be sure to ask about the monthly limited-edition cookie! It rotates regularly.

🌐 www.gideonsbakehouse.com

f www.facebook.com/gideonsbakehouse

📍 3201 Corrine Dr Orlando, FL 32803

Get carnivorous at Terra Gaucha

The Terra Gaucha Brazilian Steakhouse in Tampa brings authentic "Churrascaria" to central Florida, and you will be begging for more after each helping of their delectable beef, pork, lamb, seafood and chicken. They have fantastic sides and a tremendous salad bar, and the "Brazilian Barbeque" they offer is steeped in rich South American tradition. The "Gauchos" cowboys of yore would be impressed with the dynamic flavors of the meats there, and the charcoal wood and rock salt used in preparation are always just right. This is a meat-lover's dream and we highly recommend this spot should you find yourself spending some time on the Gulf Coast.

_____

🅕 www.facebook.com/terragauchasteakhouse

📍 1108 South Dale Mabry Highway, Tampa, FL 33629

25

Taste the islands at Jerk Flavas Restaurant

Since 2016, owners Willo and Paulette and their kids have been serving up some of the tastiest jerk chicken, oxtail and curry goat in all of Florida. However, the duo running the show have been in the game for more than 20 years, and they know how to deliver top-tier Jamaican flavors; after all, they learned how to cook on the island itself. This was rated the top fast-food restaurant in Cocoa for good reason, and they promise to delight guests from near and far with their tasty meals. This spot is conveniently located right off I-95, so give them a holla if you are making your way down the east coast during your Florida vacation. It will most definitely be worth it!

jerkflavasrestaurant.com

www.facebook.com/JerkFlavasRestaurant

935 School St., Cocoa, FL 32922

26

Savor the 'gator at Happy's Bayou Bites

Po'boys, shrimp, gumbo, chicken and alligator (yes, that is right, alligator!) are just some of the southern delights you will find at Happy's Bayou Bites. They will come to you or you can stop in to see them, but either way you are sure to be satisfied by their tasty comfort food. They aim for unique, charming and community-driven, and they deliver on all of those fronts. They have award-winning food served with a smile, and the warmth of the Florida sun pales in comparison to what you will get from proprietors Mark and Happy. These "Bites" are great, and if you happen to float through Dunedin you should stop in and say hello!

🌐 happysbayoubites.com

f www.facebook.com/happysbayoubites

📍 431 Skinner Blvd, Dunedin, FL 34698

27

Delight in the dishes at Victoria & Albert's

Located at Disney's Grand Floridian Resort & Spa, this is simply one of the finest dining experiences you will find either on Disney's properties or anywhere beyond. They offer modern American foods infused with ingredients from all over the planet, including Japan, Italy and Russia. All of them blended with local seafood, North Carolinian poulet rouge and much more! If you are looking for a really special night out with your best guy or gal, book a seat in the secluded Queen Victoria Room. Chef Scott Hunnel and the entire team at Victoria & Albert's really are a cut above, and you will be in awe of the experience they have waiting for you there. Notable menu items include the Spanish octopus and the Iberico ham and sherry vinaigrette.

🌐 www.victoria-alberts.com

📍 4401 Floridian Way, Orlando, FL 32830

Try a treat at William Dean Chocolates

Looking for somewhere sweet to bring your beau in the Clearwater area? William Dean Chocolates is the place to do it; they offer little tastes of heaven with their hand-made artisanal desert offerings designed to delight your tastebuds. The shop has been delivering some of the best chocolates in the area since 2007, and their experience and expertise show in the products. They also boast that their chocolates are made in small batches without the use of any preservatives. Simply put, it is pure chocolate bliss. Come for the delicious desserts and stay for the amazing presentation. You absolutely will not be left disappointed after a trip to William Dean.

---

www.williamdeanchocolates.com

www.facebook.com/WilliamDeanChocolates

2790 West Bay Drive, Belleair Bluffs, FL 33770

29

Sample the sea at the Indigenous Restaurant

The Indigenous Restaurant is focused mainly on sustainable seafood, but all of their seasonal American cuisine is a cut above. Their close relationship with local artisans, farmers and fisherman is evident in their always-fresh foods. This is a place focused just as much on creating a better "food system" as they are creating better food. As far as location is concerned, they are located in historic Towles Court, a scenic and storied section of downtown Sarasota. The unique charm of the area is infectious, and this is a great region for some true R&R. Also, Indigenous Restaurant has indoor and outdoor seating year-round, so you will be able to enjoy whatever setting tickles your fancy should you find yourself there.

f www.facebook.com/IndigenousSarasota

📍 239 S. Links Ave., Sarasota, Florida 34236

Greektown Taverna

We want all of your international culinary bases covered in this guide and that includes Mediterranean delights from Greece, too! If you happen to be traveling down Florida's east coast and find yourself north of Daytona Beach, you will find some of the finest gyros and baklava in the entire Sunshine State at the Greektown Taverna. Their expansive menu hits on all the Greek classics and you will feel right at home in their warm, welcoming establishment. Plus, you will undoubtedly leave satisfied by their generous portions! This is a great spot to hit up after catching a NASCAR race, soaking up some beach sun or simply if you are looking for some great Greek food. North-central Florida visitors, go get something good there!

🌐 www.greektowntaverna.com

f www.facebook.com/GreektownTaverna

📍 150 North Nova Road Ormond Beach, FL 32174

31

The ZAUQ Indian and Pakistani Cuisine

Family-owned, The ZAUQ Indian and Pakistani Cuisine is dedicated to providing the best service in town. This is also another place with a tremendous menu of beef, chicken, lamb, fish vegetables and phenomenal naan—all at a great price, too. They also offer a pretty neat customizable menu for events, so if you are planning to have anything catered while you are enjoying your time in the Tampa Bay area, this is a great place for both affordability and flexibility, and we give it our full endorsement. Pair a meal at the ZAUQ Indian and Pakistani Cuisine with something to get your creative juices flowing; the bold flavors they offer up will have you itching for a challenge!

zauqtampa.com

www.facebook.com/ZauqTampa

4040 W Waters Ave., Tampa, FL 33614

Go organic at The Green Room Cafe

Organic food never tasted so good! The Green Room Cafe emphasizes organic products, and it's conveniently located in breezy Cocoa Beach. The Green Room Cafe boasts top-notch smoothies, sandwiches, wraps as well as vegan and vegetarian options and alternatives for both gluten and wheat products. This place truly offers something for eaters of every dietary persuasion, and we highly recommend this spot should you have any special dining needs. If you are really looking for a healthy, refreshing treat, we suggest one of their amazing Acai Bowls. These bad boys are packed with anti-oxidants and vitamins; they're exactly the kind of meal you and your travel companion will want to recharge and re-energize while vigorously adventuring around central Florida.

🌐 www.thegreenroomcafe.com

ⓕ www.facebook.com/CocoaBeachGreenRoomCafe

📍 222 N. 1st Street, Cocoa Beach, FL 32931

33

Get the royal treatment at Chatham's Place Restaurant

With live music, fine dining and an atmosphere that encapsulates all the best parts of central Florida living, Chatham's Place Restaurant is remarkable. With Mr. Bob Rose tickling the ivories and top-tier sommelier Peter Freeman managing the restaurant's expansive wine selections, you will feel like a duke and duchess after a night at the Chatham's Place Restaurant. Whether you indulge in the fresh seafood, the mouth-watering filet mignon, or one of their delicious soups, you will not leave hungry or disappointed. Needless to say (though we will say it anyway) this is a first-class date night-spot that you and your partner will be talking about long after you board your return flight. Amid a pretty incredible collection of places to eat in Orlando, Chatham's place is right at the top of that list.

chathamsplace.com

www.facebook.com/chathamsplace

7575 Dr. Phillips Blvd. Orlando, FL 32819

Let Nonno's feed you the Sicilian way

Nonno's Italian cuisine is rooted in Sicilian traditions and cooked with an obvious love and passion for food-craft. They highlight their Tortellini di Leo and Pollo di Stefano, but the menu is loaded with Italian classics that are nothing short of masterful. The team there grinds out each day's work to meticulously ensure every meal for every guest is on point. This is the type of food and service you would expect from a restaurant named after "grandpa," and you will certainly be glad you hit this one up with your best guy or gal. The atmosphere here matches the passion of the cooks, and it is for that reason this is a perfect date night destination.

🌐 www.nonnositalianrestaurant.com

f www.facebook.com/nonnositalianrestaurant

📍 1140 E Altamonte Dr #1018, Altamonte Springs, FL 32701

35

Enjoy the nightlife at Mathers Social Gathering

When we talk about the stellar Orlando nightlife scene, this is the sort of place we are referring to. Its exposed brick and deep wood color are elegant and tasteful, just like their menu offerings. Mathers is hidden away above an old 1800s-era furniture store, and you will definitely feel like you are drinking in another century should you find yourself there. The entire place is designed around the concept of social gathering and they aim for both comfort and sophistication; we believe they deliver on both. While you're there, don't forget to try the "Bathtub Gin" and the "Bourbon Berry" both fantastic drinks. Mathers Social Gathering is all about presentation and vibes, so grab your travel companion, pull up a chair, and soak in this old-timey throwback gem.

🌐 www.mathersorlando.com

f www.facebook.com/mathersorlando

📍 30 S. Magnolia Ave., Orlando, FL 32801

Dive into a bowl at Michi Ramen

This place specializes in nice, light fare that is perfect for unwinding after spending a hot summer day exploring Tampa. Their Asian-inspired menu focuses on quality ingredients and sassy flavors, even if it is not as big as some of the other restaurants you might try. What they do, they do well. We especially like the curry seafood ramen and the spicy stamina ramen; both brought serious, dynamic flavorings that all worked well together. Give Michi Ramen a chance after boating in the bay or pushing your heart rate up. This is a great spot to take it slow, relax and enjoy some fantastic ramen delights!

———————————

🌐 www.michiramenfl.com

f www.facebook.com/Michi-Ramen-101447414815461

📍 18025 Highwoods Preserve Pkwy, Tampa, FL 33647

37

Nibble some noms at Viet-Nomz

Viet-Nomz offers really tasty Vietnamese cuisine in a sleek and modern way. Located just north of Orlando in Winter Park, they are a great casual spot you could turn to as you hustle and bustle your way up and down central Florida looking for wildlife and sea creatures. At Viet-Nomz, presentation is the name of the game, and everything you order looks like a piece of artwork. This is a great way to get some satisfying Vietnamese food on the go, but we do highly recommend the flexibility of the "build your bowl" option. Of course, if you are looking for something already put together, try the surf and turf; it is a true slam dunk!

🌐 vietnomz.com

f www.facebook.com/vietnomzfl

📍 7581 University Blvd, Winter Park, FL 32792

38

Island Fin Poke Company-Winter Springs

Hawaiian-style poke borne from farm-to-fork—you won't get anything frozen and thawed out there—the Island Fin Poke Company prides itself on serving the freshest fish and produce in the game. The menu is creative, the food is memorable and you will be begging them for their incredible recipes by the time you are all finished. The salmon and ahi tuna are always a hit and the catch-of-the-day is always exceptional. This is a nice spot to hit if you are staying anywhere in the Lake Jesup region north of Orlando. Give them a chance if you want that the best fresh seafood flavors from 4,600-miles away brought right to your vacation destination.

www.islandfinpoke.com

www.facebook.com/Ifpcwintersprings

1450 Tuskawilla Rd. Suite 108, Winter Springs, FL 32708

39

Sample South America at Taste of Peru

The fried sweet plantains at Taste of Peru justify their titular name; they are absolutely fantastic and you will feel like you are sitting in South America as you enjoy these perfectly cooked masterpieces. We also loved the Chupe de Camarones—a creamy broth with shrimp, vegetables, egg and more all topped with cilantro an oregano—and if you are a fan of Latin cuisine you will be a fan of Taste of Peru. We know Orlando has no shortage of options when it comes to dining and entertainment, but when it comes to Peruvian cuisine, you will be hard-pressed to find a better spot. The "taste" at Taste of Peru is just right!

🌐 www.tasteofperu.net

f www.facebook.com/Taste-of-Peru-Orlando-Peruvian-Restaurant-431626856934395

📍 9521 S Orange Blossom Trail Ste. 117A, Orlando, FL 32837

40

Cool down at the Ice Dreammm Shop

The flavors there are like a "dream," and the cozy atmosphere is everything you are looking for after a long day in the central Florida sun. Grab you partner and treat them to a nice game of checkers while you laugh over a tasty cone or cup. Yes, the ice cream is great there, but so too are the music, hilarious videos, and overall cheerfulness of the staff. Everything at the Ice Dreammm Shop is made onsite and there is absolutely no artificial coloring in any of their ice cream. Ice cream and Florida go hand in hand, so grab your best traveling companion by the hand and hurry down to the Ice Dreammm Shop if you happen to need a refreshing treat between Land O' Lakes and Tampa.

icedreammmshop.com

www.facebook.com/icedreammmshop

23912 State Road 54 #2 Lutz, FL 33559

41

Refresh yourselves at Meshi Ya

They say there that food is a way to bond with others, and that this reality spans county, culture and geography. We love the sentiment, and we love the offerings. At Meshi Ya, you can expect them to bring that same dedication to service to your bubble tea dining experience. All of their ingredients are as fresh as their incredible takes on classic recipes, and you can always expect to be treated like royalty when you eat there. Palm Bay is a beautiful south-central destination on the Atlantic coast, and if you are adventuring in the many natural and wildlife sections there, Meshi Ya is the perfect place to flip through your photos and enjoy a nice tea with your travel partner.

meshiyatogo.com

www.facebook.com/Meshiyafl

2150 Harris Ave NE, Palm Bay, FL 32905

Spoon up the flavor at Thai House of Orlando Restaurant

In Thailand, knives and chopsticks are not normally needed to eat meals. To that end, you will likely be eating with a large spoon and a fork if you find your way to the Thai House of Orlando Restaurant; the meats there are prepared in nice, neat bite-sized morsels just as they are in Thailand itself. Whatever you try there is going to be tasty no matter what size it is served, but we especially recommend the satay appetizer or the Thai House duck for an entrée. We love authentic international dining experiences, and you will be hard-pressed to find one more so than at the Thai House of Orlando Restaurant. Give this one a go for all you Disney guests looking to get off-campus for a meal.

🌐 www.thaihouseoforlando.net

🅕 www.facebook.com/Thai-House-Of-Orlando-116407811716613

📍 2117 E Colonial Dr, Orlando, FL 32803

43

Savor the flavor at H'ours Creole Smokehouse

H'ours Creole Smokehouse uses locally grown produce to supplement its incredible surf and turf offerings. The attention to detail they put into their menu comes off clear as a sunny Florida day, and you will be blown away by their culinary creativity. They have indoor and outdoor seating and a pretty neat bar, too. The vibe at H'ours Creole Smokehouse is relaxed and the atmosphere makes it the perfect place to wrap up a chill beach day. Should you be passing through Tarpon Springs—a great destination rich with history and culture—let the team there delight your tastebuds and lift your day. Note that menu items especially noteworthy are the "Drunken Scallops" and "Pork Parmesan."

www.hourscreole.com

www.facebook.com/hourscreolesmokehouse

310 E Tarpon Ave., Tarpon Springs, FL 34689

Yum Yum Hot Pot AYCE

Hot pot Chinese cooking is a beautiful, delicate way to prepare a meal, and you and your partner are going to have a delightful time indulging in this niche culinary experience. You will be served a delectable boiling broth of your choosing to dip, dunk, and drop your raw ingredients into—those range from meats to vegetables, tofu, noodles and more—and then watch as your food elements come together to create the perfect meal. Of course, the dipping sauces are fantastic, too, and you will want to be sure to get a healthy heaping of them with each morsel. At the Yum Yum Hot Pot, take your date night (and your meal) into your own hands with this cool, clever dining experience.

yumyumhotpottampa.com

www.facebook.com/Yumyumhotpot

11301 N 56th St., Unit #6, Temple Terrace, FL 33617

45

Mom's Restaurant Haitian Cuisine and Bakery

When it comes to good eating, Central Florida has all the international bases covered; from the Caribbean islands to Greece, Japan, Italy and more, you really can take a virtual tour of the globe while vacationing in the Sunshine State. To that end, Mom's Restaurant Haitian Cuisine and Bakery provides a neat combination of traditional bold island entrees with exceptional desserts at their top-tier bakery. From the poulet to the cabrit, everything at Mom's hits the palate exactly right. This is a great stop in Tampa for travelers on the go looking to get in a quick fix of something saucy before hitting the town. We love this place for a lot of reasons, but the uncompromising dedication to capturing the very best of Haitian cuisine has got to be at the top of that list.

🌐 momshaitiancuisine.business.site

📍 11900 North Nebraska Avenue Suite #1, Tampa, FL 33612

Tally ho at The Friar Tuck

A rare find in the region, The Friar Tuck brings a unique twist on British culinary classics. For more than 20 years, the establishment has worked toward ensuring guests have the best experience possible, and they have definitely been able to do just that with their committed and hardworking staff of cooks and servers. The Friar Tuck actually imports many traditional items from the U.K. itself so your experience there will be nothing short of authentic. We recommend the Scotch eggs, chicken pot pie and Cornish pasty for those you looking to get the best of what they serve "across the pond." Hit up this spot after a day relaxing on beautiful Lake Apopka or one of the area's many other breathtaking lakes.

🌐 www.thefriartuck.com

f www.facebook.com/clermontfriartuck

📍 Cagan Park Avenue, Clermont, FL 34714

47

ShouFi MahFi
Mediterranean Grill

New York transplants who brought their irresistible Mediterranean cuisine to the greater Orlando area are the reason central Florida vacationers get to experience the exceptional offerings of the ShouFi MahFi Mediterranean Grill. This place rocks, plain and simple. They preach a passion for cooking, dedication to perfectly crafted family recipes and determination to deliver great meals every time as the reasons for their success. We recommend trying the Bocas Fried cauliflower wrap, falafel platter or a delicious spinach roll if you are looking for a great dinner for two. Make sure you save room for dessert, though; the harissa is absolutely out of this world.

www.shoufimahfi.com

www.facebook.com/ShouFiMahFi

8379 S John Young Pkwy, Orlando, FL 32819

Get serious about your meat at Kres Chophouse

At the Kres Chophouse, you will be served up classic items prepared with a new and modern twist. The building's architecture is stunning, and the classic décor will take you back to the sultry 1930s. They have tons of original artwork on display and the atmosphere is really something to see. Most importantly, though, they are not fooling around when it comes to their meats! The prime beef they use is aged on the premises and custom cut for your order. Of course, if you and your special someone want to try some seafood instead, they can take care of all your underwater culinary needs with some of the freshest coastal catches in Orlando. They boast a professional and committed staff who know how to take care of their guests as well. Take your best guy or gal here for an especially special night out.

🌐 www.kresrestaurant.com

f www.facebook.com/KresChophouse

📍 17 W Church St, Orlando, FL 32801

Better Than Sex – A Dessert Restaurant Orlando

This intimate restaurant definitely hits the spot both on taste and on atmosphere. It will feel like you are back in the speakeasies of yesteryear while you and your partner enjoy chocolate, house-made cocktails, and caramel-rimmed wines. A stunning backdrop of the downtown skyline and beautiful Lake Ivanhoe create the setting for a date night at this award-winning restaurant. Every day feels like Valentine's Day at Better Than Sex, as they specialize in romance and intimacy. But be warned: with only 13 tables, you are definitely going to want to make a reservation if you are a planning a night there. This is a must-hit spot for romantics looking for some alone time with their partner.

🌐 www.betterthansexdesserts.com/location/better-than-sex-orlando

f www.facebook.com/betterthansexkw

📍 1905 N. Orange Ave, Orlando, FL 32804

Experience craftsmanship at Strong Tower

The Strong Tower Vineyard & Winery (a certified Florida Farm Winery) is the product of years of planning, and it really shows. They grow extremely specific grape varieties that are chosen to create exactly the flavors they are looking for. All of this equals a masterful group of wines to choose from for you and your special travel companion, and they all have something to offer. They specifically boast of their delicious sweet blueberry, strawberry, and watermelon wines that are all extremely well crafted. The notes are subtle and well balanced. The Strong Tower Vineyard & Winery is a perfect spot for a daytime dalliance with your partner just off Florida's gulf coast; give them a try and enjoy the goods!

🌐 www.strongtowervineyard.com

f www.facebook.com/Strong-Tower-Vineyard-Winery-123666204424385

📍 17810 Forge Dr., Spring Hill, FL 34610

51

Mama mia, Pizza Mia

Florida may not be New York or Chicago when it comes to pizza, but there are still a few hidden gems scattered throughout the state and this is definitely one of them. Simply put, this is the best pizza in Vero Beach. They have wings, they have Chicken Parmesan, and they have specialty pies that will have you kissing your fingers after each bite. This is a full-service spot that has some great wine and beers, too, so enjoy an authentic Italian meal with your amore at this east coast staple. We love Pizza Mia after a long day swimming in the beautiful Atlantic Ocean; you will be sure to work up an appetite, and they will be sure to take care of that!

🌐 www.pizzamiavb.com

ⓕ www.facebook.com/PizzaMia82

📍 1115 21st Street Vero Beach, Vero Beach, FL 32960

Wake up to the wines at Siesta Key Wine Bar

Siesta Key Beach is a great place to relax, in general, and there are few better ways to enjoy the beautiful area than to sample some of the absolutely delicious wines at the Siesta Key Wine Bar. They have as many as 40 types of wine for you to choose from, and you can sample them in a flight, by the glass, or of course, by the bottle. They also offer a pretty great VIP wine club that you can take advantage of if you are staying in the area for a little while. Another great amenity, too, is the free parking they have to help ease your travel troubles. All around, you will definitely not be disappointed by the Siesta Key Wine Bar's performance!

🌐 siestakeywinebar.com

ⓕ www.facebook.com/siestakeywinebar

📍 5138 Ocean Blvd, Siesta Key, FL 34242

53

Taste the heat at Kimchi Korean Restaurant

Kimchi delivers on Korean food done right. The savory beef katsu looks as good as it tastes, and the entire operation stands out for both its presentation and its flavor. The udon, japchae, grilled fish and pot stew are all also great options if you are looking for some lighter fare. This is another great spot in the Lake Jesup region, and you and your partner will appreciate the authenticity of the offerings, the size of the portions and their dedication to using only the freshest ingredients. Give the Kimchi Korean Restaurant a try if you are in the mood for some spicy Korean food at an affordable price.

🌐 orlandokimchi.com

f www.facebook.com/OrlandoKimchi

📍 7 Alafaya Woods Blvd. #1000, Oviedo, FL 32765

Spice up your day at Mana Mana Middle Eastern Restaurant

See where the Middle East comes to middle Florida in full splendor. Be it the hummus, the kebabs, the salads or shawarma, Mana Mana has everything you would expect from a Middle Eastern eatery and then some! They boast visitors and clients from all over the world including Egypt, Israel, Russia, Hungary, Mexico and more. The reason these visitors keep flocking there? The food is simply out of this world. Stop in if you are looking to spice up an evening after a chill day exploring beautiful Clearwater, or if you are just looking for a little punch with your dinner. We loved it there for exactly those reasons and so will you!

---

www.manamanarestaurant.com

www.facebook.com/ManaManaClearwater

530 Park Street, Clearwater, FL 33755

55

Beautiful baked bites at the Astoria Pastry Shop

These homemade Europeans desserts are delectable, and they are the perfect way to start any sunny Florida day. You will be able to smell the delicious baked goods even before you get through the doors as the pastry chefs there are always up bright and early to make sure everything is just right for incoming Floridians and tourists alike. The space itself is extremely warm and welcoming, and for the days when the sun is not shining so brightly, you will be able to enjoy your baked treat inside their cozy establishment. This is the type of place that will have you wanting to get up at first light looking for a fresh breakfast and some hot coffee. Astoria is the spot for all your baking needs if you are staying in the west Tampa Bay area.

🌐 astoriapastry.com

𝗳 www.facebook.com/belleairbakery

📍 560 Indian Rocks Rd. N. Belleair Bluffs, FL 33770

Grab lunch at the Sulphur Springs Sandwich Shop

The Sulphur Springs Sandwich Shop offers a thoughtful, comprehensive menu with sandwiches stuffed to the max that are full of fine meats and delicious sauces. Sulphur Springs itself is a great place to take in some nice architecture, and while you are there you can mull over the beauty of the historical buildings while enjoying a fantastic sandwich. This place is dedicated to quality; they actually roast their own turkey and beef, and bake their own breads daily. They boast no nitrates and no preservatives in the offerings, either. You will truly appreciate the attention to detail that this place has, and it's a must stop-destination if you are craving something savory.

🌐 www.tampasandwichshop.com

f www.facebook.com/tampasandwichshop

📍 9000A N Florida Ave. Tampa, FL 33604

57

Sample what's sizzling at Bocas Grill Orlando

Bocas Grill is a masterful example of a Latin American fusion restaurant that really hits the mark on creativity and selection. From authentic Venezuelan empanadas to the fantastic Bocas burger, this place has a massive menu that literally spans an entire continent of history, culture and tradition. The grill emphasizes diversity of flavor, thoughtful menu crafting, and generous servings that will delight you and your companion all night long. Located in southwestern Orlando, this Bocas Grill Orlando is nestled neatly in between several of the lakes central Florida is known for. Hit them up after a day of kayaking on the lake or exploring the gorgeous wildlife for some fantastic food.

bocasgrill.com

www.facebook.com/bocasgrillrestaurant

7600 Dr Phillips Blvd, Suite 22, Orlando, FL 32819

Try Venezuelan delights at Arepita Beach Daytona

Arepita Beach is the spot for Venezuelan cuisine in the famed Daytona Beach area of east central Florida. The meals are tasty, the vibe is fun, and the overall experience will be really great for you and your special travel companion. And, for those who might need it, ask about their gluten free options (they have a nice selection of those as well). This is a great spot for an exotic dinner after a day of soaking up that hot Florida sun. We highly recommend this joint if you are craving some tasty Latin American cuisine in a pretty neat looking building. Also, see about the scenic patio seating!

🌐 www.arepitabeachfl.com

f www.facebook.com/Arepitabeachdaytona

📍 174 N Beach St., Daytona Beach, FL 32114

Barkada Bowl Poké and Filipino Food

If you are a seafood and poké lover then this is certainly the right the joint for you! The money-maker at Barkada Bowl Poké and Filipino Food is their magnificent sauces; most notable are the Hawaiian Teriyaki and the tangy Citrus Ponzu. Always fresh, this is a great way to bring some of the eastern hemisphere over to Florida's east coast. The Barkada Bowl Poké and Filipino Food is the perfect spot for a healthy meal after a long day of relaxing at the beach! We love it there and are betting you will as well!

barkadabowl.com

www.facebook.com/barkadabowl

8010 N. Atlantic Ave. Suite 5, Cape Canaveral, FL 32920

Affordably delicious gyros at Papa Sabz

The Papa always delivers at this counter service Mediterranean joint in Casselberry. This is the Greek and Mediterranean spot for those staying north of Orlando and looking for some spanakopita, falafel and, of course, gyros as they meander about central Florida. For some outstanding side dishes, too, the pita and Tzatziki sauce or the tabouli are great lighter fares for those trying not to go overboard. No matter how you slice it, Papa Sabz offers quality food for the Floridian on the go with great service and at affordable prices—these are their hallmarks. You'll be glad you stopped in on your way to and from the Orland theme parks!

papasabz.com

www.facebook.com/PapaSabz

500 State Rd 436, Suite 1020, Casselberry, FL 32707

61

Go mad for Mad Dogs Hot Dogs

There is something about having a good hot dog on vacation that is almost a requirement for any traveler. If you are looking for the best dogs in the Venice area while vacationing your way through the middle of Florida, we suggest Mad Dogs Hot Dogs. Their specialty offerings are unique and delicious—The Icy New Year Splitter Dog masterfully blends cream cheese, creamy horseradish sauce, sriracha, and hot red pepper relish, while The Doginator Dog comes right at you with bacon, barbeque sauce, and roast beef complementing each other nicely. These are tasty and creative, and they're the perfect lunch for a break from your hike on Tamiami Trail. Stop by Mad Dogs Hot Dogs and get yourself the vacation staple you and your travel companion will no doubt be craving!

🌐 www.maddogshotdogs.com

f www.facebook.com/Mad-Dog-Hot-Dogs-108553752542831

📍 2059 Tamiami Trail S., Venice, FL 34293

Taste the islands at YAH MON Caribbean Restaurant

This is the place to get your authentic Caribbean dining experience in central Florida. One of the hottest spots in Tampa Bay, give them a try if you are looking for a little bit of heat. Their seafood, chicken and goat are always on point and their curry flavorings will all but transport you to the Caribbean islands themselves. We highly recommend the baked tilapia and the mango salmon, especially if you are a seafood lover. This is a highly rated spot and a perfect date night location if you are looking to spice up an evening with bold flavors and a lively atmosphere.

🌐 yahmontampa.com

f www.facebook.com/YahMonTampa

📍 301 W Platt St. Ste C Tampa, FL 33606

63

Bring lots of napkins to Git-N-Messy BBQ

The name says it all at this fantastic barbeque joint; between the brisket, homemade jalapeño sausage, pork, catfish, and chicken, you will be sure to be covered in one sauce or another by the time you finish eating. Good barbeque in the south is pretty much a given, but Git-N-Messy is something special just north of Orlando. The truth of the matter is that this place takes barbeque seriously. Whether it is the surf they are serving up or the turf on which you are chowing down, you are going to be treated to something savory and delicious at Git-N-Messy. Come prepared to leave full and be sure to use an extra wet napkin or two after dinner!

www.facebook.com/GitNMessybbqOrlando

855 E SR 434 Winter Springs, FL 32708

Share a glass at Bohemios Wine & Beer Tapas Bar

What is a more perfect date night than sharing a bottle of wine over some delicious tapas? At the Bohemios Wine & Beer Tapas Bar, that is exactly what you will get to do! The place is gorgeous, the food is outstanding, and the mood is just right for a fun, stimulating evening out after a day of boating, hiking or hitting up Florida's many theme parks. They say that Bohemios is the engagement of an "unconventional lifestyle," usually in the company of others, in pursuit of the same artistic and spiritual experiences. This entire concept is the perfect encapsulation of how you will feel after a night out at the Bohemios Wine & Beer Tapas Bar. You will leave alive and invigorated!

🌐 srqbohemios.com
f www.facebook.com/BohemiosSarasota
📍 3246 Clark Rd. Sarasoata, FL 34231

65

Try a zesty bite at The Florida Key Lime Pie Company

The name of the game there is "refreshing." Be it the pie, the homemade ice cream or the saltwater taffy, this is a dynamite destination to hit up if you are looking for a breather from an aggressive day of fun in the sun. Just south of the Cape Canaveral Air Force Station, you will not be disappointed by this top-flight key lime pie. Also, where else are you going to get pie on a stick? And, for you cheesecake lovers, the flavors of the Caribbean marble chocolate offering are out of this world. If you are looking for some zesty and delicious dessert offerings while visiting the "Space Coast," this is the spot to hit!

🌐 www.flkeylimepies.com

f www.facebook.com/TheFloridaKeyLimePieCompany

📍 102 Dixie Lane, Cocoa Beach, FL 32931

Relax at The White Heron Tea & Gifts

There are a lot of places you could go to relax whilst galivanting about central Florida, but perhaps one of the most relaxing places of them all is White Heron Tea & Gifts. They are aiming for a spa experience in a resort setting, and they really do deliver on all of that in addition to having some really nice teas. This is an immersive experience that also comes with some delectable food pairings to really round out the engagement. For a nifty, unique afternoon outing in beautiful New Port Richey, White Heron Tea and Gifts is the place you want to be.

🌐 www.thewhiteheronfl.com

f www.facebook.com/thewhiteheronfl

📍 6228 Grand Boulevard, New Port Richey, FL 34652

67

Learn how good vegan food can taste at Dharma Fine Vittles

This Orlando vegan hot-spot is growing in popularity, with easy-access right in Orlando. It's not often that a total-vegan food concept opens in the state of Florida, which is why Dharma Fine Vittles is starting to really put themselves on the map. And even though it's vegan, don't let that fool you, their menu has the likes of: Brew Burgers, Heirloom T.L.T., Big Burritos, Hail Kale Salad, Biscuits n' Gravy, Florida Fried Green Tomato, and the list goes on. The savory scents and remarkably subtle flavors will give you a culinary experience that goes far beyond what you may think of as vegan cuisine. Certainly, an adventurous culinary endeavor, this is a fun food destination to surprise your sweetheart with on date night.

🌐 dharmafinevittles.com

ⓕ www.facebook.com/dharmafinevittles

📍 2603 E South St, Orlando, FL 32803

Enjoy a taste of sunshine at Kafé del Puerto

This little slice of paradise has some of the best pork chops, fried chicken and ground beef on the "Space Coast," and you will be glad you gave them a try after exploring all the great wildlife and technological marvels in the area. This "Kafe" is as cozy and comfortable the way you will feel after enjoying some of their delicious Puerto Rican offerings and it is a neat place to have a relaxed dinner with your special travel partner for a less formal date night. We loved the food and we loved the service. This is the place for traditional Puerto Rican fare on the east side of Florida.

🌐 kafe-del-puerto.business.site

🅕 www.facebook.com/kafedelpuerto

📍 7000 N Atlantic Ave., Cape Canaveral, FL 32920

69

Taste the luxury at Eddie V's Prime Seafood

If you're looking for a more elegant, high-class, and luxurious kind of evening experience, then Eddie V's Prime Seafood is surely a destination to consider. The charismatic vibes draws you in and makes you feel at home, as you sit back and savor the finest seafood and steaks in the world. This is the place to enjoy elegant Chilean sea bass, perfectly broiled lobster tails with medallions of succulent filet mignon, and more. Paired with the best wine you can access, as well as live jazz in the V lounge, you can gaze at the curated artwork and décor while you savor one of the best high-class seafood experiences in the state. If you're unsure of your visit, you can always book a virtual visit starting today. Check the link below!

🌐 www.facebook.com/EddieVsPrimeSeafood

📍 7488 W Sand Lake Rd, Orlando, FL 32819

📍 4400 W Boy Scout Blvd, Tampa, FL 33607

CHAPTER FOUR
81 ideas to Try in Central Florida

L ooking for something more adventurous? We've found dozens of great activities for you to try in the heart of the Everglade State. From thrilling physical activities that will get your pulse racing to quieter things you and your partner can do together; we've got things for you to try in Central Florida that will make your vacation a special one.

01

Sculpt your perfect vacation at Charlie Parker Pottery

We all know the inherent romance of pottery (thanks Hollywood!). But, even in real life there is something magical about the way the clay feels, the soothing sounds of the studio, and the satisfaction of creating something beautiful with your own hands. We think that you and your partner are going to love this pottery class for the simple reason that Charlie Parker and his team are pros' pros, and you will be in good hands with them should you find yourself looking for a creative date night experience in the Saint Petersburg area. There is never a bad time to make art, so if you are looking for a creative outlet during your central Florida travels, we found one for you here.

🌐 www.charlieparkerpottery.com

f www.facebook.com/Charlie-Parker-Pottery-143278235683807

📍 2724 6th Ave. South, Saint Petersburg, FL 33712

Try some straight shooting at Farewell Firearms

Blow off a little steam at a Farewell Firearms Training site near Lake Wales. They teach everything from the basics all the way up to defense and tactical classes as well as offering an opportunity to enter into competition. You may not think the gun range is a typical date spot, but the adrenaline and excitement from the firearm experience can be both exhilarating and educational. The professionals here are top-flight and you will immediately be more comfortable with your weapon once you start your class. We are all about new experiences when it comes to your central Florida vacation, and this is definitely the route to go if you are looking for something unique to do. Hit up Farewell Firearms before a night on the town and take aim at some great memories.

🌐 www.farewellfirearms.com

f www.facebook.com/FarewellFirearms

📍 Lake Wales, FL 33853

03

Carve some memories at the Florida School of Woodwork

We are always up for learning a new skill or hobby, so if you and your partner are thinking about learning something unique, give the Florida School of Woodwork a visit. They say that there is something special about bare wood and making something beautiful with it, and we completely agree. The classes there are clear and helpful, and you will feel like a master crafter in no time under the tutelage of the great instructors there. The workshop itself is almost as beautiful as the things you are going to be crafting, too, so there really is no reason not to hit them up if you are staying in Tampa.

🌐 www.schoolofwoodwork.com

f www.facebook.com/SchoolofWoodwork

📍 1609 N Franklin St., Tampa, FL 33602

Take to the waters at Discovery Cove

Every couple needs to swim with dolphins together, right? These gleaming gray hides and cheerful, mischievous dispositions of these magnificent animals has earned them a place in everyone's hearts. Quite possibly one of the most intelligent animals in the sea, if not the planet, spending time with dolphins is an unforgettable experience. There is no better state for such engagement than the state of Florida. Make your way over to Discovery Cove in Orlando to swim with dolphins or fish. You can also elect to play with delightful sea otters, feed colorful tropical fish, and engage in a slew of other animal activities that you will want to share with all of your friends and family.

🌐 www.discoverycove.com/orlando

📘 www.facebook.com/DiscoveryCove

📍 6000 Discovery Cove Way, Orlando, FL 32821

05

Fly high at Orlando Flight School

What better way to see famed Orlando, Florida than flying high above it during a flight lesson at the Orlando Flight School? This is a great way to really shoot some adrenaline into your vacation and see if you have what it takes to pilot an aircraft. This school is approachable and accessible, and they will do what it takes to make sure you and your partner have the experience of a lifetime. Try a one-time "Discovery Flight," which will put you in the cockpit (with an experienced pilot, of course) and get you flying right away. And, if you are so inclined, they have all the tools needed for you to take your flight school experience to the next level. Give them a try and see how much fun you could have hanging out with the birds!

🌐 orlandoflightschoolfl.com

f www.facebook.com/OrlandoFlightSchoolfl

📍 400 Herndon Ave., Orlando, FL 32803

Camp in style at Fort De Soto Park

The sprawling Fort De Soto Park Campground has all the amenities you would expect, plus some really neat extras you don't get at any old campground; they have washers, dryers, up-to-date restrooms, a store, and even their own, on-site disposal stations. Located just minutes from Tampa Bay and Clearwater Beach, this is a prime spot to rest your weary head after a long day of kayaking, biking, or strolling about the beautiful west coast of Florida. If you are looking for a nature-filled trip to Florida's great outdoors, you can camp in style at the Fort De Soto Park Campground. You will be hard-pressed to find a better place in the area.

🌐 www.pinellascounty.org/park/camping.htm

ⓕ www.facebook.com/PinellasCountyNews

📍 3500 Pinellas Bayway South, Tierra Verde, FL 33715

07

Aim for the heights at Dynoclimb

"Exhilarating" and "spectacular" are the two best ways to describe an afternoon at Dynoclimb. Indoor rock climbing is equal parts challenging, exciting, and straight-up fun. The interior design at Dynoclimb is really something to behold, and the challenges you will encounter there will give you and your special travel partner a real run for your money should you want to scale up there. They say that your experience there will be "dynamic in movement, primal in nature;" we could not agree more. Also, ask about their other fitness offerings like their yoga classes for a more relaxing way to enjoy the space. This place is "dyno-mite" all the way around.

🌐 www.dynoclimb.com

f www.facebook.com/dynoclimb

📍 528 S. Woodland Blvd., DeLand, FL 32720

Ride into the sunset at Hidden Palms Ranch

Take your lover on a romantic horseback ride through some of the most stunning country Central Florida has to offer. You will likely find some eagles, some ospreys, and maybe even a hawk as you trot through this gorgeous land. In the summertime, you will be awestruck by the wild sunflowers strewn about; and in any month, the ancient oaks will have your jaw on the floor. The guides at the Hidden Palms Ranch are great, and the horses are truly magnificent. And, to fully round out the experience, you will be afforded plenty of time for a few photos with your four-legged pal and a chance to toss them a few treats. This is the perfect date-day excursion for anyone staying in the Lake Monroe area.

🌐 www.hiddenpalmsranch.com/orlando-trail-rides

f www.facebook.com/hiddenpalmsranch

📍 1410 Oakway, Sanford, FL 32773

Find your need for speed on the waves with Extreme Jet Ski

Extreme Jet Ski of Orlando offers affordable jet ski fun in sunny Kissimmee. The jet skis they rent are cool-looking, and you will be looking pretty sweet yourself should you decide to rent with them. Cruise the choppy waters of Lake Cecile on some of the finest watercraft you can find and enjoy every inch of nautical kick. This is a good move for beginners and adventurers alike, and you won't need a reservation to get on a boat. Keep in mind, though, riders born after Jan. 1, 1988 will need to pass a water safety exam and watch an instructional video. Budget the needed time if you fit into that category!

🌐 www.extremejetskioforlando.com

f www.facebook.com/ExtremeJetSki

📍 4836 W. Irlo Bronson Memorial Hwy., Kissimmee, FL 34746

Bodyslam boredom at the Manor Professional Wrestling Dinner Theatre

If you're in the mood to try something really different, or if you want to treat a husband/boyfriend to something he is going to love, then consider a dinner at the Manor Professional Wrestling Theatre. Created by Bryan Smith, who founded the pro wrestling dinner on a Kickstarter campaign in 2021, the wrestling theater features local professionals who compete once per month for what's known as the Manor Medallion. Where else can you watch a live wrestling act in person while enjoying a delicious dinner consisting of wrestling-inspired dishes, like the Head Lock Green Salad or the Drop Kicking Veggie Medley. It's certainly not something you're going to find anywhere else.

🌐 www.manorprowrestling.com

ⓕ www.facebook.com/manorprowrestling

📍 1875 Silver Spur Ln, Kissimmee, FL 34744

11

Float through the waters with Wild Willy's Airboat Tours

Florida's famed everglades are a remarkable, one-of-a-kind natural feature that are truly a blessing for the entire region and state. Team up with Wild Willy's for a great way to explore this natural wonder: an exciting airboat tour that will leave you breathless. You can glide across this gorgeous landscape in an awesome passenger boat that will delight the explorer and the gearhead in both you and your partner. There is no bad time to be on the water anywhere in Florida, but the striking vistas created by the angling sun on the everglades are truly exceptional. Bring a camera and be awestruck by what you will find on one of Wild Willy's wild rides. They are fun and affordable.

🌐 www.wildwillysairboattours.com

ⓕ www.facebook.com/WildWillysAirboatTours

📍 4715 Kissimmee Park Road Saint Cloud, FL 34772

12

Feel feral at the Cheetah Hunt

If you have ever wondered what it's like to be a jungle cat on the prowl for its lunch, this is the place to find out. The Cheetah Hunt ride at Busch Gardens Tampa Bay takes you high atop the park and then sends you racing down and right through a gorge and beyond with this 4,400 behemoth. Cheetah Hunt is the park's longest attraction and thrill ride, and you will not want to miss even a second while riding it. There is absolutely no shortage of things to do at Busch Gardens, but this ride is a must-hit for any coaster enthusiast, thrill seeker or animal lover. We had an amazing time here and we have no doubt you will, too. Hop on the hunt and stalk that prey!

🌐 buschgardens.com/tampa/roller-coasters/cheetah-hunt

ⓕ www.facebook.com/BuschGardensTampaBay

📍 10165 McKinley Dr, Tampa, FL 33612

13

Pedal your way to fun with Celebration Bike Rental

If you want to see the many great offerings that the charming Town of Celebration has for residents and visitors alike, hop on a bike and take one of the 90-minute self-guided tours offered from this nifty bike rental shop. The bikes are clean, modern, and in tip-top shape. Celebration is quaint, elegant and classy featuring beautiful architecture, bountiful wildlife and lots of great places to eat and shop. Look for waterways, trails, or just meander the streets on one of their rentable bikes. This is a great way to mix in some cardio with your traveling companion amid all the eating and drinking you will be doing while away. There is never a bad time to get in some exercise, even while touring beautiful central Florida!

🌐 www.bookabiketour.com

f www.facebook.com/CelebrationSurrey

📍 700 Bloom Street, Kissimmee, FL 34747

Float away with Painted Horizons Hot Air Balloon Tours

If you are looking for a way to scope out all the great stuff going on in Orlando in one fell swoop, try taking a ride with Painted Horizons Hot Air Balloon Tours. They love hot air balloons, and it shows! In a balloon, you can see all the happenings going on in Orlando, Kissimmee, and even the Disney World region. Painted Horizons sends balloons up every day of the week so long as the weather permits. And, they also offer a great "couples only" experience that is perfect if you want to enjoy a more intimate experience with your travel partner. Painted Horizons Hot Air Balloon Tours is special, and you are really going to love what they are selling.

🌐 www.paintedhorizons.com

📘 www.facebook.com/PaintedHorizons

📍 12559 State Rd. 535, Orlando, FL 32836

15

Try not to get eaten at Jurassic Park River Adventure

This is a classic take on a classic movie. The signs on the course all said "restricted" and you should have listened! Actually, it's better when you break the rules a little bit. This is a crazy good time for you and your beau, and you are going to want to make sure to hold them close as the dinos close in! There are lots of great rides at Universal Orlando, but this is definitely one of the top offerings.

🌐 www.universalorlando.com/web/en/us/things-to-do/
rides-attractions/jurassic-park-river-adventure

f www.facebook.com/UniversalOrlandoResort

📍 6000 Universal Blvd., Orlando, FL 32819

16

Get extreme with Gator Paintball

Woodsball, Ghost Town or a giant "inflatable field" are just some of the courses you can try out at Gator Paintball Extreme. This place has more than 30 acres of land, fully developed in service of paintball shooting. This Hudson destination is just north of Tampa, and if you're hanging out in the area and want to get your marksmanship on, this is the place to do it. They have a great staff, exceptional referees, and offer food and drink on site. Even if you have never played before, the team there will show you all the ropes and help you get the hang of it all. One important note at Gator Paintball Extreme: they only allow house paint, so plan accordingly!

gatorpaintball.info

www.facebook.com/gatorpaintball

11122 Houston Avenue, Hudson, FL 34667

17

Hit the trails at Doris Leeper Spruce Creek

Hitting these trailheads is a great way to see the east coast of central Florida just south of Daytona Beach. The ups and downs of this beginner and intermediate level track span about 8 miles of largely shaded woods, and all of it is quite spectacular to look at. They also note that the Doris Leeper Spruce Creek MTB Trailhead is part of the Flagler Area Biking club, so if you are planning on sticking around for a little while you might even consider tagging along with these active riders. Biking is a great way to offset some of the lavish eating and drinking in which we tend to indulge on vacation, so hit up the Doris Leeper Spruce Creek MTB Trailhead for some fresh air and much-needed cardio!

🌐 www.flaglerbiking.com

f www.facebook.com/Spruce-Creek-Mtb-Trail-572082766223954

📍 2194 Creek Shore Trail New Smyrna Beach, FL 32128

18

Swim for it at Dayo Scuba Center LLC

The Dayo Scuba Center is a premier Scuba diving operation located just north of Orlando. They have a great team of active trainers and divers as well as a super pro shop for all your equipment needs. We love the idea of exploring underwater, and one of the absolute best ways to do that is by learning how to Scuba dive. You and your partner will love what it looks like below sea level, trust us! Let the Dayo Scuba Center show you the ways of the water and see how much cool stuff you and your partner can find. Also, ask about their cave diving training; that is one heck of a way to get your deep-water fix in!

www.dayo.com

www.facebook.com/dayoscuba

723 Executive Dr. Winter Park, FL 32789

19

Unleash your inner artist at Art Centric Studio

Come make something beautiful at the Art Centric Studio, which is a nice to look at itself as the artwork being created there. There is tons of natural light to help lift your spirits and your creativity. You will be given a step-by-step guide with respect to what materials to use, how to use them, and even some creative ways to work around the mistakes that inevitably crop up during the art-making process. Grab your partner and see what wonders you can make! You will make art, but most important, you will make memories.

🌐 www.artcentricstudio.com

f www.facebook.com/ArtCentricStudio

📍 Dixieland Village Plaza, 1035 South Florida Avenue, Suite #180, Lakeland, FL 33803

20

Take off with Jones Brothers Air & Seaplane

Let's add another mode of transportation to our central Florida selection: sea planes. Established more than a decade ago, Jones Brothers Air & Seaplane Adventures operates a fleet of Cessna, Searey and Piper aircraft that will really impress you. They have some really cool planes to see, and the vehicles themselves are as much of a draw as the sights you will see inside them. They offer tours, charters and even flight-training for pilots and visitors. We say, why not introduce another element into your central Florida vacation and take to the skies in a Jones Brothers Air & Seaplane Adventure; you will like what you see!

🌐 www.jonesairandsea.com

f www.facebook.com/jbseaplanes

📍 210 E Ruby St. Tavares, FL 32778

21

Get wet at Clearwater Jet Ski Rentals

We Get You Wet Watersports is the perfect place to quench your thirst for adventure. There, you can rent jet skis, boats, kayaks and paddle boards to help you get your fix in. They are a great operation, and they know how to take care of customers. Being on the water is always a win, and doing it while zipping around on one of their jet skis is going to be a memorable experience for you and your partner. This is a great place in a great location; they boast no beach traffic and free parking. At Clearwater Jet Ski Rentals -We Get You Wet Water Sports you are getting fun delivered in heaps!

🌐 wegetyouwetwatersports.com

f www.facebook.com/wegetyouwetrentals

📍 1300 Cove Cay Drive, Clearwater, FL 33760

See the world at Epcot Theme Park

This is Disney's one-stop shop to show you all the best parts of the globe, the sea, outer space, and beyond with their world-class attractions, entertainment and cuisine. Perhaps the best place to eat in all of Walt Disney World, the sampling of world culture and offerings available in the back-half of the park is really something to behold. Also, keep an eye out for some really great Frozen-themed attractions. You will likely need a whole day there, so plan accordingly if you have an aggressive Disney-centric vacation booked. With new offerings constantly being added, this is simply one of the finest destinations in all of Orlando. Be sure to take your time exploring this crown jewel of Florida.

🌐 disneyworld.disney.go.com/destinations/epcot

ⓕ www.facebook.com/WaltDisneyWorld

📍 200 Epcot Center Dr, Orlando, FL 32821

23

Feel the rhythm at TaToSalsa Studio

While there are plenty of dance clubs, bars and restaurants you could take your partner for a night of dancing, the Latin dance classes at TaToSalsa Studio will help you "step" up your game big time. They offer classes in Salsa, Mambo, Bachata and the Cha-Cha, and also offer private lessons so you and your partner can really get into rhythm. We love the idea of taking a dance class ahead of a night on the town; it will help get you ready for whatever the evening might have in store. Give TaToSalsa a chance if you are looking to get in up close and personal with your partner and burn a few calories while you are at it. And, the best part is that you will have these great new moves for a lifetime!

www.tatosalsa.com

www.facebook.com/tatosalsatampa

2901 West Busch Blvd, Tampa, FL 33618

Hit the green at Orange Tree Golf Club

The Orange Tree Golf Club is a magnificent, family-owned, private course featuring 7036 yards of golfers' bliss. This is a great course for players of all skill sets, and you are sure to have a great time on these meticulously-maintained links no matter how much golfing experience you have. This course is the big time, too, as it is both a U.S. Open Local Qualifier and a state Senior Open Qualifying course. They boast a lot of great features, but avid players will especially appreciate the closing holes known only as "The Loop." This is a great course and a wonderful way to spend an Orlando afternoon. Grab your partner, grab a cart, and see who can win the day at the Orange Tree Golf Club!

🌐 www.orangetreegolfcluborlando.com

f www.facebook.com/OrangeTreeGolfClub

📍 7540 Woodgreen Dr., Orlando, FL 32819

25

Gear up for fun at Tank America

This is definitely not your average vacation destination! At Tank America you will be afforded the chance to drive an actual, real authentic FV433 Abbot tank through a half-mile course full of hills, mud holes, forest, jungle and more. You are, quite literally, going to be in the driver's seat when it comes to the action. They have 35 acres of land to play with as well as a 5-acre deep lake on site. And, if you are up for even more fun, you can give their tactical laser tag game a go as well. This takes place in a 20,000 sq. ft. building specifically crafted to fit military themes. This is probably the only date you will ever go on that features heavy military weaponry, so make sure you soak it all in while you are there!

www.tankamerica.com

www.facebook.com/tankamericafl

9150 Ellis Rd. Melbourne, FL 32904

26

Take to the stage with ClassAct Studios

Aspiring thespians, listen up! ClassAct Studios is one of the best acting schools in all of Florida, if not the whole region. This is a great place to see if you have the chops to be a Hollywood lead. You and your partner will get a kick out of the role-playing and manufactured banter you will get to do at the studio. ClassAct aims to create a safe environment for all actors to develop their skills. If you have ever wanted to give acting a shot, this is the place to do it. As far as creative date experiences go, taking an acting class is pretty high on that list; and, who knows, you may even find some hidden talent just waiting to burst out onto the scene! Give this fun, creative studio a chance to see if they can create the next Hollywood A-lister!

🌐 www.classactstudiosorlando.com

f www.facebook.com/ClassActStudiosOrlando

📍 11561 Lake Underhill Rd, Orlando, FL 32825

27

Have a colorful adventure at Urban Core Paintball

At Urban Core Paintball, get ready for some extreme fun. Bring your own gear or rent some of their brand-new equipment at this top-flight Tampa paintball establishment. They have six awesome courses for you to try out, and your heart and adrenaline will be thumping and pumping as paintballs crash and splatter all around you. This is the spot for the couple looking to get some aggression out, so decide before hand if you want to be on the same team or go head to head on the battlefield! Paintball shooting is always a good time, and it's especially fun when you can do it together. We highly recommend bringing some extra water, though; it can get pretty hot out there!

🌐 www.southtampapaintballs.com

f www.facebook.com/southtampaspaintballco

📍 3378 S. 50th Street, Tampa, FL 33619

Become an ace at Warbird Adventures

This is your one-stop-shop to become a WWII aircraft fighter pilot and also see some of the coolest military memorabilia around. Yes, you read that right; you could fly a plane at the Warbird Adventures museum! There, they offer a 100% fully hands-on flight experience in "The Pilot Maker." Add a little adventure into your central Florida vacation and see if you might have a future in flying high with this amazing aircraft. And, for those who may be a little shy to take to the sky, there is still a ton to see and do at the museum; the history alone is worth the trip. If you are staying in Orlando's southern suburbs, this is a great find for the history buff and the aspiring fighter pilot alike!

🌐 www.warbirdadventures.com

f www.facebook.com/warbirdadventures

📍 4134 Aviation Dr., Kissimmee, Florida 34741

29

Catch a big one with YACHTFISH Fishing Charters

With both inshore and deep-sea fishing expeditions available, this charter service can handle all of your St. Petersburg fishing needs. You can hit them up for a four-hour jaunt, or you could book a whole eight-hour day with them in search of grouper, amberjack, pompano, kingfish, and more. This team knows what they are doing, and they guarantee you will catch something thanks to their high-quality electronics, top-tier boats and equipment, and dedication to ensuring a good time for you and your partner. We will never say no to the open seas, and YACHTFISH Fishing Charters is a great outlet to get some saltwater air and soak up the Florida sun.

🌐 www.yachtfish.com

f www.facebook.com/YachtFish

📍 101 Bay Shore Dr NE, Slip Q12 St. Petersburg, FL 33701

Take dinner up a notch with a Cozymeal Cooking Class

Flexibility is the name of the game when you choose to book with Cozymeal Cooking Classes. There, you can book online courses, take mixology lessons, or even book a private, intimate and personalized cooking experience with one of their professional chefs. Sharing a meal together is always a romantic notion, but creating that meal with one another is even a notch above that. And, that is exactly what you will get to do if you book a Cozymeal Cooking Class. Take a night off from the crowds, excitement and hustle of the central Florida restaurant and bar scene and spend some time learning something new with your partner. It is fun, affordable, and a great way to mix up your vacation schedule.

🌐 www.facebook.com/cozymeal

f www.cozymeal.com/tampa/cooking-classes

📍 4830 West Kennedy Blvd, Suite 600, Tampa, FL 33609

31

Ride the waves with CF Watersports

If you are going to take a beach vacation to Florida, you might as well take full advantage of one of the absolute best parts of such a trip: the beautiful and refreshing open water. At CF Watersports, you will be able to rent all sorts of equipment (with fuel included) like the 2020 Stingray Deck Boat and the Crest Platinum Boat. These vessels are new, comfortable, and luxurious. This is another great way to inject some romance into your trip and snuggle up close with your best guy or gal as you sail into the sunset, enjoying the gently cool breeze. Of course, CF Watersports can also hook you up with a captain for your excursion, should you need one! Located all around the Orlando area, they can help with all your central Florida boating needs.

cfwatersports.com

www.facebook.com/cfwatersports

Greater Orlando Area, FL

Put the pedal to the metal at Orlando Kart Center

Are you and your partner feeling the need for speed? If you are, and you are in the Orlando area during your stay, hit up the Orlando Kart Center. There, you can cruise your way up to 45 MPH in their souped-up karts on a nearly one-mile long track. You will face bumps, curbs and more as you navigate your way to the finish line. This is a great way to add a little competition into your trip; let's see if you can't beat your travel companion to the checkered flag and claim the title of vacation-racing champion! Also, they offer league play for you extended stayers. This place is simply one of the best in the business for all your kart-racing needs.

🌐 www.orlandokartcenter.com

f www.facebook.com/OrlandoKart

📍 10724 Cosmonaut Blvd, Orlando FL 32824

33

Hang ten at Pure Life Surf School

If you and your partner are looking to introduce a little amphibious challenge to your vacation, give the folks at the Pure Life Surf School a ring and see if they can't teach you the ways of the waves. They will show you how to surf there, they say, but they will also ensure they show you how to surf well. The instructors at the Pure Life Surf School are top-tier athletes who have been teaching people to surf for a long time. We suggest taking a private lesson so you and your partner can learn at your own speed. Lessons are tailored to your skill set, and if you have never surfed before they will help get you up to speed in no time.

🌐 purelifesurfschool.com/contact

f www.facebook.com/purelifesurfschool

📍 2705 South Atlantic Ave., Daytona Beach Shores, FL 32118

34

Sail the Everglades with Peace River Airboat Tours & Charters

One of Florida's most defining activities is taking an airboat through the Everglades to experience some of the most unique wildlife in the U.S. With Peace River Airboat Tours & Charters, enjoy a fast-paced trip on one of the vessels that was built for pride and performance. There's no better way to get around the swampy waters of the Everglades than one of these boats, designed to glide over any combination of water, mud, and plants. With a 450-horse power machine that will whiz you around the swamp enclaves, sit back with your sweetheart and take some unforgettable photos. Their team goes above and beyond to make it a personal experience.

🌐 www.peacerivercharters.com

f www.facebook.com/PRCAirboattours

📍 4192 SW Adventure Way Arcadia, FL 34266

—— **35** ——

Soar above with
PARASAIL SIESTA

As you can tell, we love any way to get a new vantage point of the beautiful Central Florida coastlines and heartland. That is exactly what you will get at PARASAIL SIESTA. Located in gorgeous Siesta Key, they offer some of the newest equipment, boast the safest and most up-to-date features, and are bi-annually inspected by the United States Coast Guard. This place is dead-set on safety, comfort, and creating a memorable parasailing experience for all their guests. Also, ask about their boat rentals. For you romantics out there, inquire about taking one of their stunning sunset tours. Being on the water is a surefire way to guarantee an absolutely unbeatable sunset experience!

———————————————

🌐 www.parasailsiesta.com

f www.facebook.com/ParasailSiestakey

📍 1250 Stickney Point Rd., Siesta Key, FL 34242

Ride in elegance with Chauffeured Services Inc.

Ride around town in style with one of the many great vehicles offered from the Orlando Chauffeured Services Inc. These rides are sweet, and they will have you feeling like royalty as you cruise around beautiful central Florida with their five-star service. Surprise your travel companion with a romantic, elegant trip to a fancy restaurant in one of their limousines, or simply take a tour around town to see the sights while relaxing in the comfort of a chauffeured ride. This is a great play on its own, but we really love using this to get out for a romantic night of dinner and drinks. Whatever you decide to use them for, you will not be disappointed in their service!

🌐 orlandochauffeuredservices.com

f www.facebook.com/OrlandoChauffeuredServices

📍 6845 Narcoossee Rd., Suite 49, Orlando, FL 32822

37

Mix it up at the Elite Bartending School

Even wonder what it might be like to impress all your friends with top-shelf bartending skills no one knew you even had? If so, then this top-shelf bartending school is the place for you. Their rigorous curriculum is aimed at teaching you real skills that you can use, perhaps even professionally, as the focus there is on the practical necessities of the trade. They have regular courses for aspiring pros, but also offer one-time workshops where you can pick up some skills in an afternoon. They offer a lifetime membership and an open bar for practicing before and after classes, so there is definitely a lot of bang for your buck. Give this a go, especially if you are looking for something a little different from the usual Orlando theme park circuit.

🌐 www.elitebartendingschoolorlando.com

f www.facebook.com/bartendingorlando

📍 56 E. Pine St., Orlando, FL 32801

38

Take in the wide-open spaces at North Beach, Suburban Estates

They have lots of land up in the Suburban Estates, with tons of space available for ATV riding, hunting, four wheeling, and more. This is a great place to get some fresh air and just soak in your Florida vacation experience one acre at a time (they have 10,000 available for recreational usage). If you really love your experience there, you can even purchase a lot for the next time you come back! This is really unique operation and a great way to stretch a vacation week into a vacation season. We love their offerings for the vast space and for the freedom you will find there, and we think you and your travel companion will feel the same way!

🌐 www.holopawfl.com

f www.facebook.com/groups/holopawfun

📍 Holo Paw Groves Rd, St Cloud, FL 34773

39

Get creative with Painting with a Twist

Lakeland's Painting with a Twist embodies the very best of the "paint and sip" concept; they have great in-studio events, awesome private offerings and even have kits that you can use at home. Have a romantic date night—either in studio with them, or at home alone—and try something spontaneous and new. It does not really matter if you have a lot of skill, a little talent, or next to none when it comes to art prowess; there's no wrong way to paint, and you are going to have a good time either way. There is nothing quite like getting your creative juices swirling around (and a glass of wine, for that matter) and seeing what your heart and mind can whip up on canvas. We love Painting with a Twist as a full-on date night experience for you and your travel partner. Also, ask about their trivia night and paint-a-pet class as well!

🌐 www.paintingwithatwist.com/studio/lakeland

f www.facebook.com/pwatlakeland

📍 3670 Harden Blvd., Lakeland, FL 33803

See an ancient sport at Sarasota Polo Club

Polo is an incredible sport with a deep-rooted history going back millennia. They say at the Sarasota Polo Club that polo is more than just a sport, it is a community. You can be a part of that community as you join the some 45,000 spectators who sit in awe of the grace, strength and majesty of the horses and the riders. Outside of the sport itself, the grounds are suburb. They feature 130 acres of manicured landscapes, 45 equestrian estates, seven Bermuda grass fields and, of course, a regulation-sized arena for the games. Add in the all-weather training track, riding trails, and stables hosting as many as 300 horses, and you have on your hands a world-class facility. This is a great place to visit and the best spot in town to learn a new sport.

🌐 www.sarasotapolo.com

f www.facebook.com/SarasotaPoloClubatLakewoodRanch

📍 8201 Polo Club Ln, Sarasota, FL 34240

41

Climb to the heights at Cocoa Beach Aerial Adventures

For a great view of the eastern coastline, give the 45 ft. high poles at the Cocoa Beach Aerial Adventures a climb. This expansive park has 49 different challenges, seven trails and three separate difficulty levels all spanning their beautiful collection of oak trees. There are obstacles to tackle, challenges to overcome and feats of strength to show off! Take your travel companion on a fun-filled aerial adventure that delivers a slightly more aerobic daytime date, and get in some healthy exercise amid all the vacation eating and drinking about town. Cocoa Beach Aerial Adventures is a great way to have some fun, get a shot of adrenaline, and see some beautiful arboreal vistas of Cape Canaveral!

cocoabeachadventurepark.com

www.facebook.com/Cocoabeachadventurepark

6419 N Atlantic Ave, Cape Canaveral, FL 32920

Get steamy at the Solace Sauna Studio

At the Solace Sauna Studio, they say that the experience is "more than just sweating, it's a solace for the soul." Hit up this spot to enjoy the myriad benefits that the sauna offers, including detox, weight loss, improved skin complexion, stress relief, support for your immune system, and pain relief. This is a fun way for you and your partner to work up a sweat, and you will feel invigorated after a session there. All of their infrared sauna stations are private, so you will have the perfect opportunity to completely disconnect from reality for a short while at the Solace Sauna Studio. We love this experience for the health benefits and for the obvious stress relief that comes with it—after all, you are on vacation!

solacesaunastudio.com

www.facebook.com/SolaceSauna

2454 Central Ave., St. Petersburg, FL 33712

Get wet with Sarasota paddleboard company

The Sarasota Paddleboard Company offer a wide array of stand-up paddleboard services including, tours, rentals, sales and even lessons for those looking to get in some practice and learn the ways of the board. They also rent out kayaks as well. Especially of note, the tour of the Exotic Lido Mangrove Tunnels they offer is breathtaking and is fun to explore either with a stand-up paddleboard or a kayak, depending on your personal preference. In general, Lido Key is an exceptionally beautiful place to see, and making your way around it in any craft is a worthwhile endeavor. This is a great destination, and a great avenue to explore it.

🌐 www.sarasotapaddleboardcompany.com

ⓕ www.facebook.com/Sarasota-Paddleboard-Company-189625751060102

📍 Lido Key, FL 34236

Blast off at the Orlando Science Center

This award-winning, hands-on science museum is a great date-night activity if you're looking to immerse yourselves in the magic of science. For more than 60-years, the Orlando Science Center exhibits have brought science to life not just for local residents, but for visitors from around the world. The center has four floors of spectacular interactive exhibit halls, labs, and workshops, as well as an observatory and experiences that are constantly changing. Areas range from the Kinetic Zone, which lets visitors explore the fundamental forces of the universe, to a gallery which offers a fusion of art and the STEM curriculum. Be sure to check in for the changing exhibitions so you can visit the center when your favorite display is occurring.

🌐 www.osc.org

ⓕ www.facebook.com/orlandosciencecenter

📍 777 E Princeton St Orlando, FL 32803

45

Up your driving game at Orange Osceola Safety Institute

If you have ever wanted to up your road skills, the Orange Osceola Safety Institute is the perfect place to do it, as they offer personalized instructions that yield real results. Perhaps, you always wanted to learn how to ride a motorcycle but never had the time or opportunity to do so? Your central Florida vacation may be just the right time to hop on some hot wheels and let 'er rip! Of course, they also offer driving instruction for newcomers and refresher courses too, if you just want to brush up on some regular cruising skills. Whatever the case may be, this is a cool way to bulk up your motor skill set and hit the road right!

🌐 www.oosi.org

f www.facebook.com/oositraining

📍 1627 E. Vine St. Suite 102, Kissimmee, FL 34744

Capture the moment with Live Wonderful

We all take so many pictures today that we sometimes forget that it's both an art and a skill. Want to learn something new and bond with your significant other while you do it? Why not consider learning photography! Bring your Florida story to life with brand photography, portraits, and photo classes that help you capture the essence of your subject. Choose from headshots and portraits, brand photography, website and social media photography, stock images, and more as you sift through classes. Pick the one that is right for you and your date and sit back while you learn the art of photography, practicing on one another!

🌐 www.livewonderful.com

f www.facebook.com/LiveWonderfulPhotography

📍 100 Rosearden Drive Orlando, FL 32803

47

Pamper yourselves at Anna Maria Beach Resort

The Anna Maria Beach Resort is a luxury locale located mere steps from the gorgeous Gulf of Mexico. Its newly renovated amenities are as spectacular as the gulf sunsets you will get to see while staying with them. They have 31 suites available, as well as other standard and deluxe rooms to enjoy. You will get to enjoy a great pool and a great staff, and the resort's palm trees gentle sway will have you relaxed in no time. Give this a look if you are planning a romantic escape from the hustle and bustle of real life; the Anna Maria Beach Resort is the very definition of relaxing in style. This is great spot and we highly recommend it to gulf coast vacationers.

www.theannamariabeachresort.com

6306 Gulf Dr., Holmes Beach, FL 34217

Learn amazing things at the Marine Science Center

If you're ready to learn about Volusia County's rich marine life, then head on over to the Marine Science Center. The center's inhabitants and ecosystems make it a unique attraction that boasts interactive learning experiences, like the seabird and sea turtle rehabilitation exhibition. This is a hands-on facility, so you'll be in for an unforgettable experience at the teaching lab, and explore exhibit galleries, plus a natural trail that illustrates the story of marine life in Volusia County. If you're interested in enrolling in the educational programs, like feeding stingrays by hand, be sure to check out the website ahead of time!

🌐 www.marinesciencecenter.com

f www.facebook.com/pages/Marine-Science-Center/ 695593160487193

📍 100 Lighthouse Drive, Ponce Inlet, FL 32127

49

Get paddling at Shingle Creek

Located conveniently inside scenic and serene Shingle Creek Regional Park, The Paddling Center offers a glimpse into the beautiful Cyprus Forest. Especially noteworthy from the center are the two-hour guided eco-tours offered in the forest, as well as the Florida Wildlife Kayak Tour at Blue Spring. There is a lot of nature to see here, and you will be awestruck by the majesty of the forest. Slip away into the woods with your best mate at the Paddling Center at Shingle Creek, and when you are done be sure to hit up come of the other great attractions in the Kissimmee region.

🌐 www.paddlingcenter.com

f www.facebook.com/thepaddlingcenter

📍 Shingle Creek Regional Park 4266 W. Vine St., Kissimmee, FL 34741

Bury the Hatchet in Tampa

They say this is great place to spice things up with your partner as you can bring out that inner lumberjack and show off your fantastic axe skills; we wholeheartedly agree. This is a fun night with a lot of great people and an atmosphere that is lively and fun. It's not as hard as it looks to fling an axe across the room, and you will be sure to be pelting bull's-eyes in no time at all! Bury the Hatchet also offers league play for those on an extended stay, or you can just come for a session and see what you can do with a little bit of practice. And this is a great survival skill to have—you can never be too prepared for what might come!

🌐 burythehatchet.com/axe-throwing-tampa-fl

f www.facebook.com/bthtampa

📍 939 Oakfield Dr, Brandon, FL 33511

51

Glide through the waters with Canoe Escape, Inc.

Tampa's finest locale for bird watching, kayaking, canoeing and photography, they offer a few hours or even a full day of exploration. See what is hanging around this 16,000-acre preserve, which also includes the many beautiful scenes of the Hillsborough River. If you look closely, you will be able to see some seasonal wildlife staples including ibis, deer, turkey, wild hogs and much more. You can take one of their kayaks and canoes yourself, or perhaps seek one of their guided tours. Whatever experience you are looking for you will find it with Canoe Escape. And, watch out! You may even come across a few 'gators hanging out on the river's logs!

🌐 www.canoeescape.com

f www.facebook.com/CanoeEscape

📍 12702 N US Highway 301, Thonotosassa, FL 33592

52

Take a leap of faith with Jump Florida Skydiving

We have talked about a lot of great ways to see central Florida; you could see if from a hot air balloon, helicopter, under water, on the lake front and more. But, above all that (perhaps both literally and figuratively) is on the way hurtling toward the ground while skydiving. At Jump Florida Skydiving you will be able to see Orlando, Tampa, St. Petersburg and more like you have never seen it before. This is, perhaps, the ultimate adrenaline rush; we recommend this one for you and your traveling partner should you be looking for a real thrill while vacationing Central Florida. Give them a try if you are willing to take your vacation experience to the max! They are great for first-timers, too.

🌐 jumpfloridaskydiving.com

f www.facebook.com/jumpfl

📍 9002 Paul Buchmman Hwy, Plant City, FL 33565

53

SwimSRQ: Swimming Lessons in Sarasota

If you are going to be touring the Florida coastlines and visiting its many lakes, there is a good chance you are going to want to take a dip in them to cool off. Should you not feel confident about your swimming ability, let the folks at SwimSRQ: Swimming Lessons in Sarasota help you brush up on your backstroke and make sure you are "swimming" your best life. Here, they will teach you safety and survival skills, proper technique and impart their love of the water to all of their students. The instructors here are friendly and knowledgeable, and they will be able to show you everything you need to know to maximize all the wonderful waterways central Florida has available.

🌐 www.swimsrq.com

f www.facebook.com/swimsrq

📍 Sarasota Sports Club, 3600 Torrey Pines Blvd., Sarasota, FL 34238

Take a break at DayDreams Day Spa

Treat yourself to an ultimate relaxation experience at the DayDreams Day & Med Spa in Brandon for an afternoon fit for a vacationer. They boast that their unique sensory therapies are results-driven and we are inclined to agree! This is a perfect pre-night-out activity for you and your travel partner; you will both be in another world after enjoying their offerings. These award-winning massages start with an "opening scent" and optional scalp massage. After that, you will be treated to one of their many choices of massage styles. A turn here will put you in the right mindset for the rest of your night and trip. We highly recommend this relaxing experience.

---

www.daydreamsdayspa.com

www.facebook.com/DayDreamsDaySpa

658 Oakfield Dr., Brandon, FL 33511

55

Get in touch with your wild side at the Animal Kingdom Lodge

This is perhaps the premier destination for travelers looking to sleep amongst the animals while vacationing in central Florida. While the Animal Kingdom theme park is itself a wonder, so too is this incredible resort hotel featuring more than 200 hoofed animals wandering freely in four giant, lush savannas. They have beautiful pool areas and stunning art on display; plus, you will be treated to all the great hospitality Disney is known for delivering. Simply stated, this place is amazing, and we think it is one of the premier destinations in all of Orlando. If you want a truly one-of-a-kind lodging experience, book a stay at the Animal Kingdom Lodge. Where else can you wake up to a giraffe knocking on your window?!

🌐 disneyworld.disney.go.com/destinations/animal-kingdom

𝖿 www.facebook.com/WaltDisneyWorld

📍 2901 Osceola Pkwy, Orlando, FL 32830

Hit the mark at Central Florida Archery & Hunting Club, Inc.

This place really hits the mark when it comes to a great all-around archery and bow-hunting experience. The service is great, and you will learn a ton about the exciting artistry of archery. The experience is geared toward learners of every skill level, and you will be hitting bull's-eyes in no time with the guidance of their first-rate coaches. For those so inclined, you will also be given a chance to learn some great bow-hunting tips. You and your special someone will be shooting better than Cupid after a few trips to the Central Florida Archery & Hunting Club! Give them a try if you are staying north of Orlando during your stay.

centralfloridaarchery.net
www.facebook.com/centralfloridaarchery
423 E Keene Rd Apopka, FL 32703

57

Get dirty with Revolution Off Road

They boast being central Florida's top off-road attraction destination, and with good reason. There are 230 acres for visitors to explore, and there is a ton of stuff to see as you weave your way through their self-guided adventures. Perhaps the biggest draw is their eight-wheeled "Mucky Duck" amphibious vehicle which goes over ponds, lakes, and land. This is a unique experience that any gearhead is going to want to see. Of course, they also have quads, four-wheelers, and buggies as well, should you want to take a more traditional approach to your off-roading experience. Everything about this place is cool, and if you are staying anywhere near Clermont you are going to want to give them a visit.

🌐 www.revolutionoffroad.com
f www.facebook.com/RevolutionATV
📍 4000 State Road 33, Clermont, FL 34714

Get wet at the Orlando Watersports Complex

Looking for something active? Check out this boat and cable park operation that provides visitors with fantastic watersport choices. It's safe, healthy, and environmentally friendly for those looking to experience the water in a monitored environment. As one of the largest cable wakeboard parks in the United States, and one of the most recognized watersports complexes in the world, this is a great place to satisfy your watersports curiosity. You can try water-based activities here that you might not get to do elsewhere, with a minimum of experience. Activities include cable sports, an aquapark, boating, group events, lessons, and more.

🌐 www.orlandowatersports.com

f www.facebook.com/OrlandoWaterSportsComplex

📍 8615 Florida Rock Rd Orlando, FL 32824

59

Sink a hole-in-one at Pirate's Cove, matey

There is a reason the Pirate's Cove Adventure Golf course was voted the best in Florida; it is because it really is! Everything from the hole design to the landscaping and spot-on pirate theme is top-tier craftsmanship. Recently renovated, you will be blown away by the time and effort that went in to creating this exceptional themed miniature golf course. And, for what you are getting, the prices are just right. Challenge your partner to a head-to-head putting showdown and see who can best navigate the waterfalls, pirate dungeons, and sunken ships at the Pirate's Cove Adventure Golf course. Just be sure to stay on the greens; you definitely don't want to get lost among the thieving buccaneers!

🌐 www.piratescove.net

fb www.facebook.com/PiratesCoveAdventureGolf

📍 8501 International Dr, Orlando, FL 32819

Catch the winds at Sailing Florida Charters & Sailing School

For all your sailing, fishing, touring and yachting needs, Sailing Florida Charters & Sailing School has you covered. With them, you will be able to see everything from Key West to Fort Jefferson, Marco Island, Clearwater, and more. Who knows what spectacular marine life you might see while sailing around the greater St. Petersburg area? Also, this is a great place to learn how to sail yourself, should you be interested in a more robust nautical lifestyle. And, ask about their romantic private cruise offerings that show off the exceptional Tampa Bay skyline. Toast yourself and your partner with some champagne or wine, and enjoy some delicious treats as you tour around the spectacular Florida coastline.

🌐 www.sailingflorida.com

f www.facebook.com/sailingfloridacharters

📍 501 Fifth Avenue NE, St. Petersburg, FL 33701

61

Relax at Caladesi Island State Park

Yes, it might seem like you are always on a beach when exploring Florida, but really, what could be worse than that? The Caladesi Island State Park is a low-key beach option where you can enjoy the beauty of the sandy shore while kicking back and getting away from the hustle and bustle of tourists. It's lesser known to people visiting from out of state, and provides some quieter beaching locations for you and your loved one. It's a great place to enjoy a secluded date, just the two of you.

🌐 www.floridastateparks.org/parks-and-trails/caladesi-is-land-state-park

f www.facebook.com/CafeCaladesi

📍 1 Causeway Blvd Dunedin, FL 34698

Play to win at
Arcade Monsters

This is the largest arcade in Florida, so you know you will have plenty to do and play should you be in the Oviedo area just south of Lake Jessup and have a hankering for some gaming. In fact, no matter where you are in Central Florida, the arcade gamer in you might want to make the trip there. This is premier gaming destination with loads of classic games, pinball machines and virtual reality games. You and your best guy or gal are going to want to warm up your thumbs before shipping off to Arcade Monsters. See which one of you hits the high score and wins the prizes there! This is a fun night for both you and your inner kid!

🌐 www.arcademonsters.com

f www.facebook.com/thearcademonsters

📍 15 Alafaya Woods Blvd #111, Oviedo, FL 32765

63

Clearwater Beach Scooter and Bike Rentals

One of the Gulf Coast's prized destinations, Clearwater Beach never looked so good as it does from the gas-powered golf carts, couple's cars (we are looking at you two...), cruisers and bikes offered from Clearwater Beach Scooter and Bike Rentals. They also have kayaks, paddle boards, and even jet skis, so there is something for adventurers of every kind there. Why not save some gas by leaving your car in the parking lot as you scoot about the beachfront in one of the many sweet rides from Clearwater Beach Scooter and Bike Rentals? Enjoy the Florida sun right, and let the breezy Clearwater air reinvigorate you and your special companion.

🌐 www.beachscooterandbikerentals.com

f www.facebook.com/scooterbikerentals

📍 619 Gulfview Boulevard, Clearwater Beach, FL 33767

Find your knight in shining armor at Medieval Times

Chivalry, bravery, courage, and nobility are among some of the best features at Medieval Times Dinner & Tournament; of course, there is great food and delicious libations, too! Queen Maria Isabella is welcoming guests into her royal court for a feast of roasted chicken, sweet buttered corn, tomato bisque soup, and more while you watch her knights show off their incredible strength and skill. You can also choose from some soft beverages and vegetarian meals as well, if that pleases you. Medieval Times Dinner & Tournament is a surefire way to nab some historical entertainment, rousing excitement, and get a hold of tons of old-fashioned fun for all the lords and ladies gallivanting through the Sunshine State.

www.medievaltimes.com
www.facebook.com/MedievalTimes
4510 W. Vine St., Kissimmee FL 34746

65

Hit the water with Paddleboard Orlando

Paddleboard is a great way to simultaneously explore new places and get in some welcomed vacation cardio exercise. At Paddleboard Orlando, you can get a look at some stunning waterways and also get a taste of the beautiful "Old Florida" section near Wekiva Island. The springs at Wekiva Island are spectacular, crystal clear, and definitely worth the price of admission. Paddleboard Orlando also boasts 35 years' worth of experience in the hospitality and watersports field, so you know that you will be treated right should you choose to spend your time there. Hit them up if you are staying anywhere between Lakes Jessup and Apopka; they are good at what they do, and you will be glad you did!

🌐 paddleboardorlando.com

f www.facebook.com/PaddleboardOrlando

📍 1014 Miami Springs Drive, Longwood, FL 32779

Climb like a monkey at TreeUmph! Adventure Course

This is the place for daring, high-flying acrobatic adventures. Built on a 14-acre piece of land, which amounts to approximately 10 football fields, you are going to find everything from wobbly footbridges to ziplines, suspended logs, and a whole lot more. You know we love mixing in adventure and athletics with the usual fare of riding and dining your way through Central Florida, and the TreeUmph! Adventure Course is definitely the way to do it. They have six adult courses to stimulate your mind and body and each of them has a little something different to offer. Give them a try before heading out to one of the many great restaurants in the area.

🌐 www.treeumph.com

f www.facebook.com/TreeUmph

📍 21805 E. State Road 70, Bradenton, FL 34202

67

Speed your way to Dade City Raceway

For another great way to zip around central Florida, hit up the Dade City Raceway. Motor cross is equal parts fun, challenging and competitive, and it is a great way to go head-to-head with your travel partner with some fast-paced racing action. At Dade City Raceway, riders of any skill level can participate, and you do not need to have any real experience with motor cross to have a good time. Stop in for great service, well-kept tracks, and an all-around pleasant experience. Also, for more serious riders, they have league play as well, should you want to test your racing skills against some other riders.

dadecitymx.com

www.facebook.com/DadeCityMX

36722 State Rd 52, Dade City, FL 33525

Take in the acrobatics at the Lakeland Water Ski Club

The team at the Lakeland Water Ski Club puts on a real-deal show; the acrobatics displayed in their water ski performance are really quite elegant, and the skiers are on point every time. Their award-winning shows are the stuff of legend, and you and your partner will be in awe of what they can accomplish with so little to work with. Give the ski club a visit if you are staying in the Lakeland area and are looking for a show that's just a little different from what you might be used to!

🌐 lakelandwaterskiclub.org

f www.facebook.com/Lakeland-Water-Ski-Club-112899962161373

📍 920 Lake Hollingsworth Dr, Lakeland, FL 33803

Peace out at Zen Glass Studio

Let's face it: glass blowing is pretty cool, and at the Zen Glass Studio you will get to make some incredible items to have forever. Sure, you could buy a souvenir anywhere on your trip, but how great would it be to make your own? The Zen Glass Studio offers private events where you can make wine and beer glasses, candy dishes, marbles, pendants and more! The process is mesmerizing, the final product is amazing, and you and your travel partner are going to love making art together. We highly recommend Zen Glass Studio for you west coast travelers looking for a creative outlet during your trip.

🌐 www.zenglass.com

🅕 www.facebook.com/ZenGlassStudio

📍 600 27th St. S, St. Petersburg, FL 33712

Skydive inside at iFLY

Although the outdoors are calling in Florida, don't forget about the incredible manmade indoor facilities that are available throughout the state! For the more adventurous couples, who wants to try free-falling together, hands held, in mid-air? If you are up for it, iFly is all of the fun of skydiving, without the risk or the hassle. Using the help of wind tunnels and professional instructors, you can experience free falling without all of the anxiety. Indoor skydiving is an astounding experience, and one you won't find just anywhere. It'll definitely make for an adventurously different date in your Florida sojourn.

🌐 www.iflyworld.com

ⓕ www.facebook.com/iFLYOrlando

📍 8969 International Dr, Orlando, FL 32819

71

Get away from it all with The Escape Game

Whether you want to explore a 1950s prison or deep space, you can find them both at the Escape Game Orlando. This hour-long adventure is chock-full of puzzles, challenges, clues and more in a game of mystery and intrigue designed to stimulate, excite and even frustrate you! What better way to bond with your travel partner than by putting your minds together to figure out the nitty-gritty details of a classic art heist? This is a wonderful date-night experience and a welcome addition to the standard range of vacation fare and activities. The staff at the Escape Game Orlando is friendly, they have tons of options to choose from, and the prices are very affordable. You'll be trying to escape, but you won't want to leave!

🌐 theescapegame.com/orlando

f www.facebook.com/TheEscapeGame

📍 8145 International Drive, Suite 511, Orlando, FL 32819

72

Push yourselves to the limit with Adventures in Florida

There is no shortage of adventure when you book with Adventures in Florida! The list of what they offer is impressive, including an amazing manatee encounter, canoe and kayak instructions, guidance from certified wilderness first responders, state Master Naturalists, and a staff that is absolutely dedicated to stewardship and the environment. This is a great place to see the gorgeous waterways in the greater Orlando area, learn a little bit about nature, and spend some time working those arm muscles as you paddle along. Nature lovers visiting the area should definitely give this a go! Pair Adventures in Florida with a hearty meal at one of Orlando's many great eateries as you are likely to be pretty hungry after all that exploring!

🌐 www.adventuresinflorida.com

f www.facebook.com/adventuresinflorida

📍 3208 East Colonial Drive #261, Orlando, FL 32803

73

Sail into adventure with CatBoat Tours

You and your partner could be cruising up and down scenic Lake Dora in a two-person catamaran should you decide to book with CatBoat Adventure Tours. With them, you will be able to take a guided tour through the Dora Canal and into beautiful Lake Eustis. There is nature and rich history on this tour and it is a great way to spend a sunny central Florida afternoon ahead of a night out. The CatBoat Adventure Tours is open year-round, so whenever you happen to be in the area—they are just north of Lake Apopka— you can book with CatBoat.

🌐 www.catboattour.com/index.php

f www.facebook.com/CatBoatTours/

📍 148 Charles Ave., Mount Dora, FL 32757

Pedal hard at Florida Cycle Park

This is the spot to hit the dirt for those central Florida visitors staying just north of Lake Okeechobee, as the Florida Cycle Park is a great place to hit up in tandem with some awesome lake-peeping. Their track-game is seriously on point, and riders who have some experience will appreciate the creativity and challenges that the Florida Cycle Park staff has whipped up for them to navigate. Again, if you want to introduce a little competition with your beau, come give the Florida Cycle Park a try. Nothing says romance like a little life in the fast lane!

www.facebook.com/florida.cyclepark

7543 NE 48th St., Okeechobee, FL 34972

75

Ride high with Cocoa Beach Helicopters

Take a trip with Cocoa Beach Helicopters and you will get to see a simply stunning look at "Space Coast" destinations ranging from Port Canaveral to Cocoa Beach, Thousand Islands and more. This is first-class way to see the sunny east coast of Central Florida in a whole new light. Hop on into the Robinson R44 N7282A (better known as "Goldie") and prepare yourselves to be dazzled by the stunning vistas. There are lots of packages to choose from, and they are all extremely affordable for what you are getting. We recommend going in all in for the "See-It-All" tour and getting the most bang for your buck. If you are looking for some sky-high adventure, this is the place to do it!

🌐 www.catboattour.com/index.php

f www.facebook.com/CatBoatTours

📍 148 Charles Ave., Mount Dora, FL 32757

Hit a home run at Ace Of Spades

Get your swing on at the Ace Of Spades Sports Baseball & Softball Academy. These indoor batting cages are awesome, and the Staff there really know its stuff. They have some great amenities, too, including air-conditioned facilities, top-tier instructors, pitching and batting lessons, strength training and more. Introduce some athletics into your central Florida vacation and see which one of the two of you can crush the pitching best! Florida is world-renowned for its baseball and softball programs, and if you want to take advantage of those programs this is a great place to do so. Batter up at Ace of Spades Sports!

www.aceofspadessports.com

www.facebook.com/aceofspadessports

500 Plumosa Ave, Altamonte Springs, FL 32701

77

Amaze yourselves with Antwan Towner Magic

Introduce some magic to your vacation (no, we aren't talking about Disney this time!) and book a show with the wondrous Antwan Towner. This guy is electric, and he knows how to work a crowd. He is part magic, part "thought seer," but 100% fun. You and your partner will be amazed at what this guy can do, and he brings heat and energy to every show. This man is a presence, and you will want to be in his!

🌐 www.antwantowner.com

f www.facebook.com/AntwanTownerMagic

📍 PO Box 75826, Tampa, FL 33675

Drench yourselves at the Typhoon Lagoon Water Park

Water park fun done the Disney way, that is what you will get at their Typhoon Lagoon Water Park. This is a top-flight water theme park that has something for even the most adventurous guests. We highly recommend the Surf Pool or the Crush 'n' Gusher—this is an especially good ride for a couple of Florida travelers looking to cool off together—among some of the other park's other great rides and attractions. The food and drinks are on the spot, the ambiance is exactly what you would expect of Disney, and this will be surefire blast for you and your travel partner should you end up there. We say, cool off in style at Disney's Typhoon Lagoon Water Park!

🌐 disneyworld.disney.go.com/parks/typhoon-lagoon

f www.facebook.com/disneyworldtyphoonlagoon

📍 1145 E Buena Vista Dr., Lake Buena Vista, FL 32830

79

Take a break at Disney's Grand Floridian Resort & Spa

This is one the finest resorts Disney has to offer, with stunning Victorian décor and all the amenities one can ask for during their vacation stay. Simply stated, this place is gorgeous, and with Disney you know you can expect top-tier service and all of that signature "magic" they are known for around the world. This homage to Palm Beach's "golden era" is just a quick ride on their complementary monorail from Disney's Magic Kingdom theme park. If you are looking for a romantic evening with your travel companion, be sure to catch their regular stunning fireworks displays over Cinderella Castle. If you can swing a few nights there while traversing the Disney theme parks, this is a fantastic place to visit.

🌐 disneyworld.disney.go.com/resorts/grand-floridian-resort-and-spa

📍 4401 Floridian Way, Bay Lake, FL 32836

Enjoy the magic of Disney World

Would this be a true Florida guide if we did not mention Disney World? Although it's a great place to bring the whole family, it's also an amazing vacation destination for solo travelers, couples, and even those planning to propose. Disney is an experience all by itself; some people make annual pilgrimages to this bastion of American popular culture. From castles, princesses, rides, delicious foods, and yummy drinks, to fun shops, art, and engaging mini pop up shows and activities, you must visit Disney World at least one time in your life. We recommend adding it to the bucket list this week.

🌐 www.disneyworld.eu

f www.facebook.com/WaltDisneyWorld

📍 Orlando, FL

81

See it all at Universal Orlando Resort

You and your travel partner will feel like real Hollywood celebrities after a few days at Universal. We have mentioned to it a number of times throughout the guide, but the Universal Orlando Resort is a massive entity with tons to offer. Between Universal Studios Florida, Islands of Adventure and Volcano Bay, there is a metric ton of things to do and see here. If you really want to get the full experience of all that Universal Orlando Resort has to offer, then you are going to want to budget for at least a weekend here. There are rides, shows, attractions, restaurants and more to see at this premier vacation spot, so make sure you plan accordingly!

🌐 www.universalorlando.com/web/en/us

f www.facebook.com/UniversalOrlandoResort

📍 6000 Universal Blvd., Orlando, FL 32819

CONCLUSION

———

Thank you for your trust in KVAALA™ brand.

In these pages we have provided you with some of the best travel and adventure destinations throughout the central region of the Sunshine State. Why leave home or travel abroad when Florida already abounds with some of the most magical terrain, establishments, and attractions around? Whether you're a Florida native or live nearby, we hope we've introduced you to something new and exciting to do, see, hear, or taste, and given you a glimpse of all you have available to you in Central Florida.

Whether you plan to travel with a boyfriend/girlfriend, a husband/wife, a date, or just a friend, this guide provides information that is perfect for couples on the go. With the information we've gathered in this guide, you can easily plan one of the most romantic getaways of your entire life no matter what you're interested in – and thanks to our painstaking research, it'll take you only minutes! Whether you're looking for bold adventure, sophisticated romance, or something quirky and new, we've got what you need to start making your dream Florida getaway a reality.

We were careful to provide a spread of mostly affordable activities, although some of the most amazing Floridian attractions that we found do come with a hefty price tag. It was our intention to provide a well-rounded guide that left nothing off of the table.

As an interactive experience, we are asking all readers to rate the book and write your suggestions in the comments. If you feel we have missed a place, we would be happy to review it and consider adding it to our list.

NEW RELEASES

Make sure you subscribe on www.eepurl.com/hcUWDb to be notified when we publish a new book with more things to see, hear, taste or try.

Made in the USA
Columbia, SC
02 May 2021